CORVETTE C5

Patrick C. Paternie

MOTORBOOKS
INTERNATIONAL

First published in 2004 by MBI Publishing Company,
380 Jackson Street, Suite 200, St. Paul, MN 55101-3885
USA

MBI Publishing Company books are also available at
discounts in bulk quantity for industrial or sales-
promotional use. For details write to Special Sales
Manager at Motorbooks International Wholesalers &
Distributors, 380 Jackson Street, Suite 200,
St. Paul, MN 55101-3885 USA

Library of Congress Cataloging-in-Publication Data

Paternie, Patrick C., 1947-
    Corvette C5/by Patrick Paternie.
      p. cm.
    ISBN 0-7603-1177-3 (pbk. : alk. paper)
      1. Corvette automobile. I. Title.

TL215.C6P38 2003
629.222'2—dc22   2003061485

About the author: "Still plays with cars," describes
Patrick C. Paternie's work as a Southern California-based
freelance writer/photographer covering new and classic
automobiles, racing, and the high-speed lifestyle that
surrounds them. Paternie's driving exploits range from
vintage Bentleys to the latest Lamborghinis on many of
the world's greatest roads and racetracks. He has worked
with racing greats like Mario Andretti, Dan Gurney, and
Phil Hill. Paternie's work has appeared in about 50
publications around the world. He is a regular contributor
to Robb Report, excellence, european car, and AutoWeek.

   Corvette C5 is Paternie's sixth book, all published by
MBI. Others include How to Restore and Modify the
Porsche 914 and 914/6, The 911 Red Book 1965-99,
Porsche 911, MINI, and Modern American Muscle.

Edited by Peter Bodensteiner
Designed by Mandy Iverson

Printed in Hong Kong

contents

PREFACE

ROUTE 66, ZORA, CHUCK BERRY, and the MULSANNE STRAIGHT

Like many of you, I was first introduced to Corvettes through the television series *Route 66*. I don't remember too much about the show except that it was about two guys named Todd and Buzz who roamed around in a Corvette convertible. For them, life was pretty simple—top down, open road, a cool-looking car, and no worries that couldn't be solved in less than 60 minutes. Who wouldn't be impressed?

Once I entered high school, I discovered that the real world was a bit more complicated than Todd and Buzz's world. Thankfully, Zora Arkus-Duntov was still at General Motors, turning out dream-world cars like 396 Sting Rays. But then a funny thing happened. Pontiac came out with the GTO and started the muscle car revolution. Suddenly you could get more thrills per dollar than with the higher-priced Corvette.

Eventually, emissions and safety legislation began to take the "high" out of high-performance cars. Corvettes also got heavier and less powerful. And they didn't seem to be assembled as well as imports like the Porsche 911.

So I forgot about Corvettes and enjoyed my Porsches—at least until I went to Le Mans with a group of fellow journalists in 1999. We were assigned to return a fleet of yellow Corvette convertibles to Paris. The cars had been used by VIPs at the race. Our trip would take two days, including an excursion to the old Grand Prix racetrack near Reims in the Champagne region. The old track had not seen a race since 1968, but the grandstands and timing tower still stood watch over the main straight, which is now a busy highway. The rest of the roads that comprised the circuit are still there and, even though there are a couple of stop signs that people like Fangio and Moss didn't have to deal with,

you can still do a high-speed lap around the old circuit. This, of course, we did—over and over—in the yellow C5s.

After that, we hit the *autoroute* toward Paris, and I experienced another magical moment. Top down, cruising across the French countryside at about 100 miles per hour, I flipped on the radio. I found a French oldies station, and the first thing I heard was Chuck Berry belting out *Back in the U.S.A.* I was racing toward Paris in America's sports car with America's rock and roller serenading me. Even Todd and Buzz would have been envious.

The trip through France in the C5 had rekindled the Corvette fever of my youth. Then along came the Z06. The 385 loud and raucous horses made it feel more like a Trans-Am racer than a street car, and it was one of the best cars in the world at any price. I fell in love with the Z06. When I returned to Le Mans in 2001, the sight of those muddy Corvettes blasting through the early morning mist stirred up patriotic pride. Good old American V-8 muscle was still a viable force in international road racing.

This fifth-generation Corvette proved to me that it was still possible for the United States to produce a car that both performed well and exuded its creator's passion for driving. For so long, I had only seen this in European and Japanese cars. Finally, American automakers were marketing a car built by enthusiasts for enthusiasts. And, amazingly, they were able to develop the C5 even while working within the monolith that General Motors had become.

When MBI Publishing Company asked me to do this book on the C5, I was excited to tell the story of not only a fine enthusiast's automobile, but also of the enthusiastic people behind it. After reading this book, I hope you will agree that the C5 is the best 'Vette yet.

acknowledgments

This is my sixth book, and although I have had some wonderful help in gathering information for past projects, I must say that the enthusiastic response I got from everyone in the Corvette family—from those at General Motors to individual car owners—has been the best I've ever received. I appreciate all the help and would like to acknowledge the individuals who stepped up to help me.

David Caldwell, coordinator for Performance Cars at GM, was a fantastic help in providing photos, offering information, and, most importantly, lining up interviews with people like Dave Hill, Tadge Juechter, and Bill Nichols. These gentlemen understand Corvettes, and they love what they do. It was great to learn that there really are still "car guys" in the car business, especially at a corporate monolith like GM. Another real car guy at GM is Jon Moss—who has one of the greatest jobs in the world because he gets to build all kinds of factory hot rods and prototypes. Thanks, Jon.

Speaking of GM, my thanks also go out to Jennifer Lesniak at the GM Media Archive and to Patty Garcia in the West Coast communications office for diligently tracking down photos and artwork. Jeff Youngs made sure that I got the new cars I needed to drive and photograph.

Thanks to Bob Bondurant for an entertaining time talking about Z06s—old and new. And I offer my gratitude to another racing hero, Parnelli Jones, for sharing his pace car remembrances.

I also appreciate the hospitality and interest given to me and this book project by Bobbie Jo Lee, Betty Hardison, and all the good people at the National Corvette Museum in Bowling Green, Kentucky. It is an entertaining place to visit even if you

Corvette, shame on you if you don't support this museum. GM helps them out, but it does not bankroll the museum's operation.

Thanks go to Chuck Spielman for providing his time and a couple of his unique Corvettes for a photo session. Steve Pasteiner of Advanced Automotive Technologies, as well as Michael Zoner and the people at Callaway Cars, also provided valuable assistance.

Dan Adovasio of the C5 Registry also gets a big nod for his time and energies.

I also want to thank my media associates. Thanks to Art Gould for providing information, promotional items, and great advice regarding the various press launches of the C5. Matt Stone and Randy Leffingwell are two of the best and busiest guys in the business, yet they always seem to have time to help me out on any project I get involved with.

Special thanks to David Newhardt for contributing a number of excellent photos. Ironically, Dave and I started working together many years ago. A wacky mutual editor once had Dave climb a tree in the middle of a cow pasture to shoot photos of a group of Japanese sports cars that influenced the development of the C5. So it was fitting that he climbed atop an airplane hangar to get shots of the Commemorative Edition C5.

Other photographers who chipped in were Tory Kooyman, Rick Scuteri, and Walt Thurn.

Thanks to my editor Peter Bodensteiner for his time, enthusiasm, and patience. And, last but not least, thanks go to my wife, Linda, for putting up with the time, attention, and whining that I devoted to this project.

Oh yeah, and I can't forget to thank Tadd and Ryan wherever

introduction

the *best 'vette yet*
almost never was

The years leading up to the actual production of the C5 version of the Corvette were fraught with enough melodrama and setbacks that the *Oprah Winfrey Show* may have been a more fitting venue for its unveiling than the "magic show" that served as its introduction.

On January 6, 1997, at the North American International Auto Show in Detroit, Chevrolet pulled off an illusionary feat. The latest Corvette was introduced almost simultaneously to automotive journalists in both Detroit and Los Angeles. Shortly after it was uncovered for the assembled press in Detroit, the car and its "driver" disappeared from the stage in Michigan and were magically transported to the West Coast. Both car and driver reappeared at the press conference in California.

The presentation was a neat trick, but it took more than sleight of hand to keep the C5 from completely disappearing well before this magical debut. Just as development of the C5 was due to begin, GM was undergoing massive financial and managerial trauma. Although the original budget of $250 million that had been approved for the C5 program in 1988 was pocket change compared to the more than $24 billion the corporation would lose in 1992, it became a target for corporate cost cutting. At one point in 1992, the Corvette engineering budget was sliced to a mere $6 million. And this number included any upgrades to the C4 that was then in production.

The fact that the C5 came to be at all is an example of how, even in a corporate labyrinth as deep and dark and twisted as General Motors was at the time, a small team of dedicated car enthusiasts could still manage to make a difference. Those who loved the Corvette found ways to keep the C5 program alive even when upper management seemed to resist the idea. They found ways to keep moving forward and were able to justify to management that the Corvette was a viable and profitable product line. They succeeded in bringing the C5 to life mainly because the Corvette has always been more than just a "product." It has been designed and built by car guys to satisfy the dreams and expectations of an equally enthusiastic and loyal customer base.

Of course, the Corvette hasn't always been a perfect car. The original 1953 Corvette may have been conceived as America's response to the sports car invasion, but even with its 102-inch wheelbase and a straight six-cylinder engine, it couldn't come anywhere close to matching the performance benchmarks set by the Jaguar XK-120. Ed Cole got 150 horsepower out of the "Blue Flame" Chevy six by adding three two-barrel carburetors, but the 1953 Corvette may have been better served if its transmission gears outnumbered its carburetors. Equipped with only a two-speed Powerglide automatic transmission (Chevy's manual transmission could not cope with the added power), the original Corvette could only muster enough acceleration to go from zero to 60 miles per hour in about 11 seconds. Top speed maxed out around 105 miles per hour. The original Corvette may have been good enough to embarrass the driver of an archaic four-cylinder MG TD , but it was no match for the more up-to-date Jaguar. With its 160 horsepower and four-speed manual transmission, the sleek British sports car was about two seconds quicker to 60 and lived up to its name by topping out at 122 miles per hour.

Things did not improve for Corvette in 1954 despite a 5 horsepower increase in power and a drop in sticker price. Chevrolet built 3,640 Corvettes that year and still had 1,500 left when the 1955 model came out. The availability of the new V-8 and a three-speed manual transmission for 1955 added a significant increase

The first Corvettes were made in 1953 and were available only in Polo White with red interior. Only 300 cars were made in Flint, Michigan, before production of the 1954 models was moved to St. Louis. There, 3,640 1954 Corvettes were made. Most of them were white, although blue, red, and black models were also offered. These 1953 and 1954 models are pictured at the Corvette Museum in Bowling Green, Kentucky.

The C4 Corvette was produced from 1984 to 1996. Before production stopped on June 20, 1996, 358,180 were made. That total accounted for nearly half of all Corvettes ever produced up to that time. Despite its popularity, the C4 had its share of structural and quality problems. *David Newhardt*

in performance, but sales dropped to only 700 units. Doubts were raised as to whether the Corvette should be continued.

The 1956 model, benefiting from a styling change and the engineering genius of Zora Arkus-Duntov, aimed the Corvette down the road to *making* history rather than the path to *becoming* history. Corvette began its drive toward achieving international status as an American performance and styling icon. It was spurred on by the technical ingenuity and affection Arkus-Duntov applied to the Corvette during his reign as its chief engineer. His term officially ended with his retirement in 1975, but he continued to monitor the car's development until his death in 1996. The Corvette would pass through three major generations of design on its way to reaching an all-time sales peak in 1979. One year after celebrating its 25th anniversary, sales hit 53,807 units.

During that period, the Corvette had to overcome various threats to its continued existence. Economic conditions, gasoline shortages, and ever-increasing regulations regarding emissions and safety equipment all endangered the future of the car. High-performance sports cars, even icons like the Corvette, are extravagant purchases, and sales suffer when the country is in a recession or when it's necessary to wait in line to buy a rationed amount of gasoline. But even when the supply of

gasoline was plentiful, there were obstacles to overcome. Corvette engineers were faced with the challenge of producing a high-performance sports car that was burdened by the weight of added safety equipment or one that had its V-8 choked by emissions equipment. The enthusiasm and passion for the Corvette of Arkus-Duntov and his successor, Dave McLellan, helped overshadow these problems so Corvette loyalists could still have the car they wanted.

By 1978, it was obvious that the time had come for a fourth-generation Corvette. The third generation of Corvette had debuted in 1968, but its chassis was basically the same as that of the second generation introduced in 1963. Planning began for the fourth-generation Corvette, now referred to internally as the C4. The car was scheduled to debut in 1983. The new Corvette would even be built in a new plant. The old plant in St. Louis, Missouri, built its last Corvette on August 1, 1981, and the new plant in Bowling Green, Kentucky, began operations on June 1 of the same year.

While it was not completely "all new," the C4 certainly did reflect state-of-the-art engineering. It featured a new suspension with fiberglass single-leaf springs mounted transversely at the front and rear, a stiffer chassis strengthened by a central backbone, a digital-readout instrument panel, and a transmission choice of a four-speed automatic or a 4+3 manual with overdrive in the top gears. To improve handling, weight distribution from front to rear was better balanced by moving the engine location back toward the center. Aerodynamic efficiency influenced the exterior design of the C4. Its drag coefficient was a finely chiseled 0.34.

Production problems prevented the C4 from being introduced on time, and it was eventually presented in March of 1983. Chevrolet did build 43 1983 Corvettes in Bowling Green, but they are considered pre-production prototypes. Because of its delayed arrival, Chevrolet decided to skip the 1983 Corvette model year entirely and launch the C4 as a 1984 model. The 1984 C4 became the second most popular model year for Corvette in history. Chevrolet, aided somewhat by the extended term of its production run, produced 51,547 1984 Corvettes.

In total, 358,180 C4 Corvettes were produced by the time the last C4 rolled off the line on June 20, 1996. Up until that date, almost half of all Corvettes ever produced were C4 models. The C4 reintroduced Corvette hallmarks such as fuel injection (originally

Corvette Chief Engineer Dave Hill poses with a Z06. Hill followed Zora Arkus-Duntov and Dave McLellan as only the third chief engineer in Corvette history. *Copyright 2003 GM Corp. Used with permission, GM Media Archive*

The C5 was originally intended to debut in 1993. When it finally made its first public appearance at the Detroit International Auto Show on January 6, 1997, Chevrolet celebrated by handing out commemorative 1/25-scale models. The miniature replicas included scale car covers adorned with the same Corvette logo that was used in the magic show that introduced the full-size car.

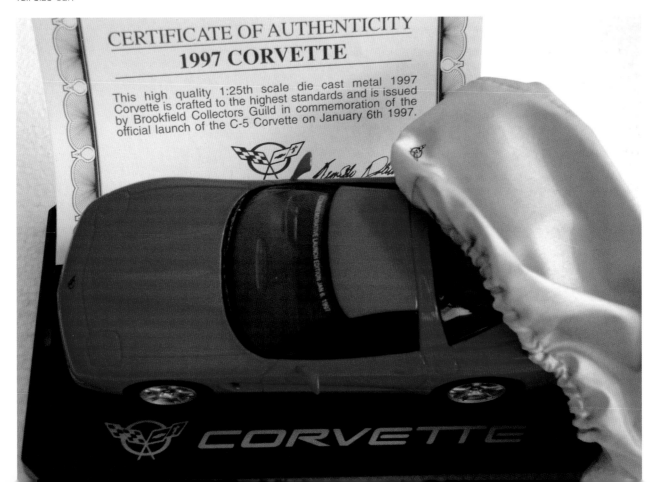

Bill Mitchell's Mako Shark I obviously influenced the design of the Corvette Sting Ray that debuted in 1963. John Cafaro said that seeing this car as a boy was the beginning of his love affair with Corvettes. *Copyright 2003 GM Corp. Used with permission, GM Media Archive*

offered from 1957 to 1965) in 1985 and the convertible (1953 to 1975) in 1986. Technical highlights included anti-lock brakes (ABS) as standard equipment in 1986, an optional console-mounted electronic switch to adjust shock absorber firmness (Selective Ride and Handling) in 1989, a six-speed manual transmission in 1989, a low-tire-pressure monitoring system in 1989, traction control (ASR) in 1992, and Passive Keyless Entry (PKE) in 1993.

The C4 family spawned candidates for the Corvette performance hall of fame. The ZR-1 "King of the Hill" model was offered as a special option from 1990 to 1995. It earned its so-briquet with an exotic DOHC, 32-valve V-8 (LT5) developed in conjunction with Lotus Engineering that eventually produced 405 horsepower. The ZR-1 package also included special wide-body doors and rear body panels to cover the massive, 11-inch-wide alloy rear wheels and P315/35ZR17 tires. In 1996, the Grand Sport name was revived for a limited run of cars that featured a 330-horsepower V-8 with high-compression aluminum heads and roller rockers that produced zero to 60 miles per hour in 4.7 seconds.

Even before these high-performance models hit the market, Dave McLellan was working on a C5 version of the Corvette.

The major issue in designing the fifth-generation Corvette was not adding more muscle. Instead, the main concern was taking the creaks and groans out of its chassis. In addition to the rattles, overall fit and finish were not up to the expectations of the current generation of more discriminating buyers. Starting in 1988, the goal was to build a Corvette that could be judged as a world-class super-performance car from the passenger compartment as well as the engine compartment.

The completely new fifth-generation Corvette, the C5, was intended to debut as a 1993 model. As such, not only was it to be a showcase for General Motors' state-of-the-art prowess in design, engineering, and technology, it was also going to symbolize 40 years of Corvette history. However, it not only missed its big birthday party by four years, but there were times when it seemed that it might never appear at all. Fortunately, thanks to the efforts of an enthusiastic band of supporters inside and outside the walls of General Motors, the C5 Corvette survived to see production. In an ironic historical twist, the C5 even hung on to become the 50th anniversary Corvette.

chapter one

OUT WITH THE OLD
and AFTER A FEW CLOSE CALLS
in with the new

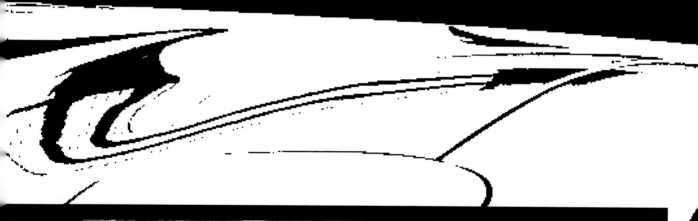

The Corvette C5 was the first all-new Corvette in history. Even the original 1953 model used many items from the same parts bin as its more mundane siblings in the Chevrolet lineup. The C5, on the other hand, carried over very few parts and pieces from its successor, the C4. The members of the C5 development team proudly puffed up their chests when pointing out that the C5 contained 1,462 fewer parts than were used in the car it replaced. The 34-percent cut in parts was due to the desire to greatly improve quality and structural rigidity while still making advances in performance and handling. Oppressive financial conditions at General Motors during the C5's development phase also demanded that, if the C5 was to be built at all, it had to be done as cheaply and efficiently as possible.

"A lot of the C5 is the result of innovative manufacturing," declares David Hill, the man who, in December 1992, took over as chief engineer of the Corvette and thus the development of the C5. "Each single-piece hydroform frame rail replaced 24 individual stampings [on the C4 frame rail], each of which came off progressive dies and fixtures to hold [it] in place so you could weld [the stampings] together. A big part of the C5 story is making the manufacturing turnaround to produce the car efficiently with a low investment so you can be successful even at a 25,000-unit-per-year volume."

The creation of innovative and efficient manufacturing methods was the brighter side of the C5 story. However, there was a darker side to the tale—one that revolves around the who and why as much, or more, than the what and how. Hill certainly played a leading role in the climactic scenes of the C5 life story, but he arrived on stage well after the drama had begun. Before solving the manufacturing problems associated with building the car, the people associated with the development of the C5 had to overcome not only the problems of the model that preceded it, but also the financial and managerial quagmire that General Motors had become by the late 1980s.

An entire book could be written about the difficulties surrounding the C5 development program—and it was. The late author James Schefter presented a detailed insider's account of the people and factors that shaped the C5 in his 1996 book *All Corvettes Are Red: Inside the Rebirth of an American Legend.* He wrote about the business, technical, and personal issues that played out inside General Motors from 1988 to 1996 and used the story of the C5 as the central theme. Schefter's book serves as a valuable research tool in tracing the C5's development and would be of interest to anyone with an interest in Corvettes.

In 1988, planning began for the fifth-generation Corvette. That year, General Motors reported a record profit of $4.86 billion—the most ever reported by a corporation.. Although its car and light truck sales declined by 7.5 percent the following year, GM's net income was a seemingly healthy $4.2 billion. Unfortunately, the bottom line was deceiving.

GM's chairman, Roger Smith, was to retire in August 1990. By 1989, the effects of Smith's corporate reorganization plans of the 1980s were starting to have an impact on sales, and that was not good news. The Chevrolet-Pontiac-Canada division lost more than $1 billion that year. Domestic sales were on a decline, and the demand predicted for GM's new line of midsize cars—Lumina, Grand Prix, Regal, and Cutlass Supreme—did not materialize. The company had invested heavily in new production plants for these vehicles, and these plants were operating at production levels geared to the optimistic sales forecasts. Their output, instead of being spread across America in customers' driveways, was stacking up in storage lots. According to Schefter, even if sales for the midsize cars had been closer to predictions, GM would have still lost up to $5,000 on each car due to cost discrepancies not disclosed during development.

The corporation lost $2 billion in 1991 and $4.5 billion in 1992 en route to going $24.2 billion in the red for 1992. After Roger Smith's retirement, the company struggled through a number of management reorganizations. There were three in 1992 alone. But when the smoke finally cleared near the end of that year, the people and the organizational structure were in place for the company, and the C5 Corvette, to start to move forward.

Dave McLellan was the chief engineer for Corvette in 1988 when planning began for the next-generation Corvette. McLellan had been in charge of Corvette since 1975, when the legendary Zora Arkus-Duntov retired. McLellan was the man who oversaw the development of the C4. This fourth-generation Corvette had been a successful sales venture for General Motors, providing a tidy annual profit of about $100 million from its usually sold-out production runs of around 25,000 units.

McLellan was given a budget of $250 million to come up with a completely new successor. That number fluctuated wildly over the following four years as the C5 program took a roller coaster ride through the halls of GM. Because of GM's financial and upper management problems, the Corvette was pushed back from being a 1993 model to a 1995 model, then to a 1996 model, and finally to a 1997 model.

The future of the Corvette was riding on the C5. In 1997, new federal regulations regarding side-impact resistance would take effect. Up until then, it was relatively inexpensive to keep producing the C4 Corvette by simply making minor tweaks and updates each year. But re-engineering the C4 to meet the new regulations would cost as much or more than bringing out an entirely new Corvette. So, in effect, no C5 meant no Corvette.

Fortunately, the C5 program came under the management of two General Motors vice presidents who understood what the Corvette meant to GM and to its loyal following. The men guiding the program were Joe Spielman and Jim Perkins.

Joe Spielman was originally in charge of the Rear-Drive Automotive Division that included Corvette. As a result of the October 1992 management upheaval, his responsibilities increased to take in the entire Midsize Car Division. Perkins was general manager of the Chevrolet division. Both men played key roles in determining the essential makeup of the C5 and keeping the program alive.

The need for developing a C5 Corvette was evident well before the impending side-impact regulations made it a necessity. The C4 Corvette may have been Chevrolet's crown jewel, but it was not without significant flaws. It had a cramped interior, virtually no trunk space, and was awkward to enter or exit because of its high, wide doorsills. But an even bigger issue was what automotive engineers call "build quality." The C4's fiberglass body panels did not fit together properly, which, in addition to causing aesthetic challenges, led to creaks, groans, and rattles when it was driven over anything but the smoothest pavement. The poor-fitting panels also allowed water to leak into the interior. To top it off, these panels also received shoddy paint coverage.

Tadge Juechter, currently Corvette assistant chief engineer, remembers interviewing with Dave Hill in 1993 for a systems engineer position on the C5 team. Juechter had been searching for a way into the "closed society" of Corvette for many years. But once Hill finally opened the door, Juechter realized he was a bit wary of joining the company.

"I had my list [of things to fix on the C4] when I came to the interview," Juechter recalls. "Even though I loved the C4, there was so much that was terrible about it. I didn't want to participate if it was just going to be a re-skin and [was going to] leave all the flaws intact."

Luckily, Juechter discovered that Hill felt the same way.

Hill says he and his C5 team "wanted the car to be every bit the high-performance Corvette that it always had been and more, but we wanted to surprise people with how many different things it can do well. We concentrated on cargo capacity, comfort, and refinement."

CORVETTE EVOLVES WITH THE SPORTS CAR MARKET

Hill, who grew up in upstate New York, had spent his boyhood fascinated by the postwar wave of sports cars like MGs, Triumphs, Jaguars, and Austin-Healeys running around the roads near his home.

He remembers the first time he saw a Corvette. "I saw one drive up to our Little League ball field. It was the first one anybody had seen. They stopped the game, and everybody ran over to get a close look," says Hill.

Hill's fascination with cars led him to pursue an engineering degree and employment with General Motors. He spent 27 years with Cadillac before accepting the position to succeed Dave McLellan as Corvette's chief engineer.

"I think my work at Cadillac prepared me to do something that the Corvette needed," says Hill. "Corvette had always been fast and tough and robust. I wanted to work on refinement—make it well rounded and the world-class sports car we wanted it to be. In the old days you had to put up with a lot in a sports car—and people did. But then they got tired of it, and sports car sales declined."

By the late 1980s, however, the sports car market was undergoing a revival. The Japanese automakers led the way with high-tech cars that emphasized luxury combined with high performance. The lead machines were the Nissan 300ZX, the Toyota Supra, the Mitsubishi 3000 GT, the twin-turbo Mazda RX-7, and the Acura NSX. These cars, except for the more expensive Acura, competed price-wise and performance-wise with the Corvette, but they were way ahead in terms of quality. So not only was it important that the C5 be an improvement over the C4, but, if it was to survive in the marketplace, Hill's team had to make sure that it was also better than this new wave of Japanese competitors.

For various reasons, predominantly escalating prices and an economic downturn in 1990, most of these cars would disappear from the market by the time the C5 finally made its debut. Only the NSX survived, and barely so, with annual U.S. sales that presently hover around the 200 mark. The C5, on the other hand, consistently enjoys sales of over 35,000 units a year.

Known as the "red car," this 1990 styling concept was designed by Tom Peters. Although Chuck Jordan, General Motors vice president of design, favored it initially, the final direction for the C5 would be a combination of this car and the "black car" of John Cafaro.

designing the c5

Dealers, journalists, owners, and other sports car enthusiasts were asked to share their opinions about how to improve the Corvette. Everyone both inside and outside General Motors seemed to agree that it was important to increase quality and comfort as well as performance in the fifth-generation Corvette. However, there were diverging opinions as to how these improvements should be carried out.

Some people favored a more radical mid-engine approach. In that camp were Jerry Palmer, the head of the Chevy 3 design studio and the person who had been responsible for the C4 design; Chuck Jordan, the vice president in charge of GM design; and Corvette chief engineer Dave McLellan. Palmer and Jordan believed that the mid-engine placement allowed them to draw up a smaller, sleeker car with a lower nose and less overhang front and rear. This meant less aerodynamic drag. From an engineer's viewpoint, the mid-engine concept was the state-of-the-art handling setup favored by exotic sports car and race car builders.

Meanwhile, GM's Advanced Vehicle Engineering group had proposed the idea of a "backbone" chassis structure consisting of one-piece side rails connected to a large central tunnel that ran the length of the car. The engine, drivetrain, and suspension would all mount onto this backbone. In effect, this chassis would contain all the necessary running gear and could conceivably be driven sans bodywork. This idea would eliminate the problematic

wide doorsills of the C4 and offer a more rigid platform than the C4's unibody construction. The problem, in Jordan's eyes, was that the backbone chassis did not lend itself to being draped in a stylish low-drag body the way the mid-engine chassis did.

The 14-foot-long, one-piece steel rails were essential to the backbone chassis architecture. But the manufacturing process for creating them had yet to be proven feasible. Still, the conservative and cost-conscious management at GM preferred this process over exotic mid-engine chassis development, which was perceived to be a waste of time and money.

The "black car" sits next to the "red car" on display at the Corvette museum. John Cafaro said that the aerodynamics of the top Le Mans cars at the time—the Peugeot 905 and Jaguar XJR8—were a big influence.

Is it real or is it Memorex? Actually this is the presentation model of the C5 that was shown to GM Chairman Jack Smith for final approval. The model, made of clay, wood, and fiberglass, has a complete interior. It is on loan to the Corvette museum by John Cafaro

All-wheel drive was also considered, but the option was voted down. The cost of development was considered too high for use on such a low-volume model as the Corvette.

After four years of on again, off again planning, GM decided to take the more conservative approach and stick with the Corvette's traditional front engine and rear drive platform for the C5. This decision led Dave McLellan to retirement in 1992.

As detailed in Schefter's book, things were as topsy-turvy in the styling department as they were in engineering. John Cafaro, who made significant styling contributions to the C4 working under Jerry Palmer, was the appointed chief designer of the C5. Cafaro traces his love affair with the Corvette back to a Mako Shark sighting at the New York World's Fair when he was eight years old. In the Chevrolet press release accompanying the C5's introduction, Cafaro claimed, "Going to the GM Pavilion to see the cars, for me, was like going to Yankee Stadium to see Mickey Mantle."

Such deep-rooted enthusiasm evidently was not enough for Chuck Jordan. Jordan, who upset GM management by driving his Ferrari to work, employed a contentious style of management. In fact, he was known as the Chrome Cobra because of his propensity to suddenly strike with caustic comments when critiquing a design. Jordan decided that Cafaro could benefit from a competition with GM's Advanced Concepts Center (ACC) in Southern California and the Advanced 4 studio of Tom Peters. The problem was that the controversial Jordan did this without telling Cafaro first. ACC, headed up by John Schinella, had come up with a "California Camaro" concept car in 1989. Jordan felt it embodied the look and emotion he was looking for when creating the latest generation of Chevy's pony car. He ordered Schinella to do a "California Corvette."

The car the West Coasters came up with in the summer of 1990 became known as the Stingray III. Wearing a sharply peaked prow and a pair of headrest fairings that enclosed a pop-up roll bar, the deep purple roadster would later stir up public interest and speculation when it was featured at the 1992 Detroit International Auto Show. The topless car struck a chord with enthusiasts and spawned a brisk business for Revell. But could it do the same as a production Corvette?

The consensus inside GM was no. First of all, the Stingray III was powered by a V-6. Everyone who knows and loves Corvettes will tell you that, while they may not all be red, every Corvette made after 1955 better have a V-8. The ACC car's styling was another problem. Besides being too impractical to build, the Stingray III was too radical a departure from the C4. One thing that the car did have was a real trunk. Thanks to the West Coast influence, the C5 would be the first Corvette convertible in three decades to include a trunk with an opening deck lid.

In 1991, Jordan reviewed more concepts for the C5. The car that was initially favored by Jordan would become known as the "red car." It was designed by Tom Peters' group. This car featured a nose similar to that of Stingray III and, with its darkly tinted, bubble-like canopy, it had an obvious jet-fighter influence.

The other car that was seriously considered was the "black car" designed by John Cafaro. It had a low nose with four tiny projector-style headlamps on a body that dramatically flared out to a Stingray-like fastback tail. Jordan, in his obstreperous style, would not totally commit to one car over the other, although Schefter says the consensus favored Cafaro's design. Jordan decided that design work should continue on the C5 using the nose of the red car along with the sides and rear of the black car. Although Cafaro would remain the frontrunner to become the C5 designer, he was still faced with competing designs from ACC as well as other internal design departments.

Jordan retired after what has become known as the "October revolution," the last round of management changes at GM in 1992. Robert Stempel, chairman of the board, was also forced into retirement during this time. This was the last of three reorganizations during that year as GM's board tried to regain control of a ship that had sprung a $24 billion leak. It's believed that the hole in GM's vessel was caused by the questionable navigational policies of people like Stempel and Lloyd E. Reuss. Reuss had been replaced as president earlier in the year by Jack Smith. Under Smith, corporate decision-making was under the control of the GM Strategy Board, which was comprised of 18 senior executives from GM's automotive business. As Jordan was literally heading out the door, his successor, Wayne Cherry, gave John Cafaro the final OK to take sole design control of what would become the production C5.

engineering the c5

In 1992, Joe Spielman set up a seven-man board called the Decision Makers. The objective of this board was to settle, once and for all, what type of architecture the C5, scheduled at the time to be a 1996 model, would use. In addition to Spielman, the board also included Corvette program manager Carlisle "Cardy" Davis, John Cafaro, and Dave McLellan. When the members of the board examined the possible architecture styles, they seriously considered three formats. The first was referred to as the "momentum architecture" because it was based on the backbone structure that had been the concept the engineering department had been pursuing for the past two years. It was a front-engine, rear-transmission model with an evolutionary body style.

The second architecture considered was a mid-engine car that offered the stylists the opportunity to create a dramatic new look for the Corvette. Although this was favored by GM president Jack Smith and Dave McLellan, it was the most complex and costly approach to developing the new C5.

The final design was called the "stiffer and lighter architecture." It was the least expensive alternative, but it involved compromises in styling, performance, comfort, and quality. It was essentially a stiffer and lighter version of the current platform.

Spielman realized that, based on GM's financial position as well as the amount of time and money already invested in the C5 program, the momentum architecture was the only way to go if the C5 was to be ready by 1996. He made sure that everyone, including McLellan, agreed that this was the path to follow. After getting a unanimous decision to this effect, he initiated a mock ceremony at the end of the decision maker's meeting during which all present joined wrist to wrist in a symbolic pact. Everyone promised not to propose any drastic changes to the path chosen for the C5.

Spielman finally herded everyone into moving in the same direction regarding the final design of the new C5. But money was still a major issue when Dave Hill took over the program at the end of 1992. The C5 development budget for 1993 was a paltry $12 million. At that time, the total amount allocated for the car's entire development period was $150 million—not enough to do a proper new generation of the Corvette. Because of the limited funding, there was still talk of making the C5 a re-skin of the C4. Chevy general manager Jim Perkins, a staunch fan of the Corvette, came up with a way of circumventing the convoluted GM budget system to provide Hill with an extra million dollars to build a C5 demonstration vehicle. The idea was to build a car that could be used for test drives in hopes of convincing upper management to raise the C5 budget back to its original $250 million level.

Perkins had already made a significant contribution to the future C5 by offering his "Billy Bob" concept of the Corvette. As opposed to the pricier coupe and convertible models already being considered, Perkins' Billy Bob was a no-frills, fixed hardtop that could be sold for $30,000. He believed that a lower-priced, basic model would be necessary to attract enough buyers to meet the volume of 25,000 cars that Corvette would need to sell each year to justify its development costs. As things turned out, the coupe and convertible attracted enough buyers on their own. Still, Billy Bob played a significant role in adding to C5 sales, but only after the concept evolved into the Z06—a metamorphosis that's detailed in chapter 4.

Hill took the $1.2 million that Perkins slipped him under the conference table and built the CERV IV, which was a C4 body over the backbone chassis of the C5. CERV, an acronym for Corvette Engineering Research Vehicle, was a tribute to the 1960 CERV I and 1964 CERV II experimental cars built by Zora Arkus-Duntov. The former resembled a single-seat, rear-engine Indy racer of the period, and the latter was a mid-engine, all-wheel drive concept that was to be Chevy's answer to the Ford GT-40. In 1989, CERV III was built as a mid-engine Corvette concept car.

"Zora built three CERVs, all mid-engine cars," says Hill. "We built the first front-engine CERV and the only one to go into production."

Actually, Hill built two CERV IVs. The original, later referred to as CERV IVa, had a six-speed manual transmission, while the follow-up CERV IVb had an automatic. Hill liked the idea of clothing the C5 chassis in a C4 body so he could drive the cars on public roads as well as on the GM proving grounds in Michigan and Arizona.

"We didn't want to reveal the styling, but we built a proof-of-process car to demonstrate the reinvented Corvette we had been scheming," Hill says of the decision to build the CERV IV. "We had to show Jack Smith [GM's president] we could not only reinvent the car but reinvent the process of manufacturing a sports car. This car helped sell the program. We took people on bumpy roads, and they would say, 'This is like no Corvette we have ever felt.'"

The CERV IV gave Perkins and Hill a great return on their million-dollar investment. It was instrumental in getting the C5 development budget bumped up to $241 million. Once the money was available, a number of alpha test cars were built. A series of beta cars was the last step in the process before production of the final version was ready to begin.

"We just never gave up," Hill declares. "We said if we show [the executive board] a truly reinvented Corvette that's also a successful business, they will support us."

Besides internal funding, there were two other major obstacles that Hill's "reinvention" of the Corvette faced. Hill was adamant that the C5 do everything at least as well as the C4—if not better. For example, a C4 could go about 350 miles on a tank of gas when driving in the city. Its range could be extended to about 470 miles on a freeway trip. The C5 would be expected to be just as fuel efficient.

One way to achieve fuel efficiency was through slick aerodynamics. Hill pressed Cafaro to continually tweak the C5 styling for the lowest possible coefficient of drag. Hill's target was a coefficient of drag of 0.29, the lowest of any current production car. The final step in reaching that goal came by smoothing out the underside of the car to decrease wind resistance.

Tadge Juechter recalls an even more challenging engineering problem related to fuel efficiency. "We didn't want to reduce the range, so we couldn't reduce the volume of the fuel tank," he says. "We took a version [of the C5] with the fuel system

A life-size replica of Dave Hill at the Corvette museum celebrates his central role in the development of the C5. Next to the ersatz Corvette chief engineer are the final presentation styling model, an LS1 engine, and one of the alpha pre-prototype test cars.

Alpha pre-prototypes were built primarily by hand using hydraulic lifts like those at the local service station. They were kept under 24-hour surveillance in a room to which only about half of the Corvette engineers had access. The alpha cars led a tough life. They were used as guinea pigs in the assembly processes and were road tested at various GM proving grounds and remote locations such as Michigan's frigid Upper Peninsula. It was an alpha car that was the first to use balsa wood in the floor construction.

Twenty-eight beta cars were built during the spring and summer of 1995. The building of the first beta car started on April 10, 1995. Beta cars were manufactured with much more precise tooling than the alpha cars and reflected the improvements realized on the alphas. The beta cars placed an emphasis on developing the quality, reliability, and desirability of the vehicle. They were tested under extreme conditions all over the world and accumulated half a million combined miles.

mounted above the axle, like many cars [have], to a clinic. It created a shallower trunk by about 5 to 6 inches. Our customers just said, 'What is that?'"

To address this problem, twin interconnecting tanks were mounted on either side of the chassis in order to leave enough space for a suitable trunk. Juechter jokes that this solution caused some fuel system engineers to retire, quit, or transfer to other projects. The system utilized a complicated series of pumps to move the fuel from one tank to the other and then on to the engine. And it had to meet strict requirements for evaporative emissions as well as prove crashworthy.

"Corvette doesn't get special dispensation," explains Juechter. "[The cars] have to meet any crash requirements that

a GM truck does, including [those] way beyond federal limits."

The other challenge was being able to prove that welding attachments to the hydroformed frame rails would work. Some wondered if there would be a problem with distortion during the MIG welding process of building up the frame.

"We solved it through 'iterative engineering,'" Juechter says. "Basically [we used] trial and error because we didn't have good computer models to tell us what a weld in the middle of the frame would do at the end."

Looking back at all the problems encountered along the way, Juechter affirms that the C5 is the result of a core group of enthusiasts who joined together and pledged, "We're going to make this happen."

Some test cars led tougher lives than others. This display at the Corvette museum shows the results of a 1994 prototype convertible crash test. This test, performed at the GM Safety Research Lab in Milford, Michigan, is a 30-mile-per-hour, 30-degree, right-angle barrier test for unbelted occupants. It is the equivalent of a 60-mile-per-hour crash with another vehicle.

bowling green, kentucky

where the american dream turns into reality
corvette factory tour and museum delivery

In 1997, a tradition was introduced along with the C5. For $490, customers could choose the R8C option. This allowed Corvette buyers to take delivery of their new cars at the Corvette Museum in Bowling Green, Kentucky. That first year, nine customers took advantage of museum delivery; today there can be as many a six deliveries in a single day. From its inception up until the middle of May 2003, 2,755 C5s first met their owners at the museum. Included with this delivery is a special guided tour of the Corvette Assembly Plant, which sits right across the Interstate 65 Connector Road from the museum. The R8C tour allows more access than the tours offered to the general public. A commemorative plaque, special doorjamb sticker, and a personalized electronic welcome on the marquee above the delivery lobby entry doors are also part of the deal. Of course, the big bonus comes after the tour. That's when it's time to drive home in a spanking new Corvette.

Corvettes have been built at the Bowling Green plant since June 1, 1981. The very first Corvettes were built in a makeshift facility in Flint, Michigan, before a dedicated Corvette assembly

This is where all of the world's Corvettes have been assembled since August 1981. The million-square-foot facility employs a little over 1,000 people. It sits just off I-65 in Bowling Green, Kentucky. Starting in 2003, a separate assembly line began building the Cadillac XLR luxury sports car. It uses the same hydroformed steel rails as the basis for its chassis.

Dollies loaded with exterior panels begin their two-mile, ten-hour-long trip through the paint shop. The panels will later be united with the frames that are being built in another area of the plant. This process is the complete reversal of the old way of assembly that attached the body panels to the frame and then sent the car to be painted. *Copyright 2003 GM Corp. Used with permission, GM Media Archive*

Panels for one specific car pass through the spray booth. The paint shop is completely automated. Two coats of primer are applied followed by two color coats. Depending on the base color, the final coat will consist of one or two applications of clear coat.
Copyright 2003 GM Corp. Used with permission, GM Media Archive

plant was established in St. Louis in December 1953. The last Corvette built in St. Louis was produced in August 1981. When the last C4 rolled off the Bowling Green assembly line on June 20, 1996, the old assembly line came down and was replaced by a new C5 line. That new line turned out its first C5 pilot production car that October. In 2003, a portion of the plant used for storing inventory was converted to a production line for the new Cadillac XLR luxury sports car.

The Bowling Green plant was originally an industrial air conditioning plant owned by Chrysler. GM expanded it from 500,000 square feet to 1,000,000 square feet. About 900 employees currently work on the C5 assembly line, which winds its way through the plant. Everything runs according to a just-in-time (JIT) process. Parts arrive from suppliers only a few days before the cars that need them are scheduled for production. All cars are built to specific orders as received from dealers. The

This is what a C5 side rail looks like before the hydroforming process begins. The rail is formed by rolling sheet steel into a tube and then closing the seam by laser welding. The tube is then bent as shown before being placed into the form that will determine its final shape. The machine is sealed, and water is pumped into the tube at pressures up to 7,000 psi. The force causes the tube to inflate to the exact contours of the form. About 15 sets (left and right sides) of frame rails are made in an hour. *Copyright 2003 GM Corp. Used with permission, GM Media Archive*

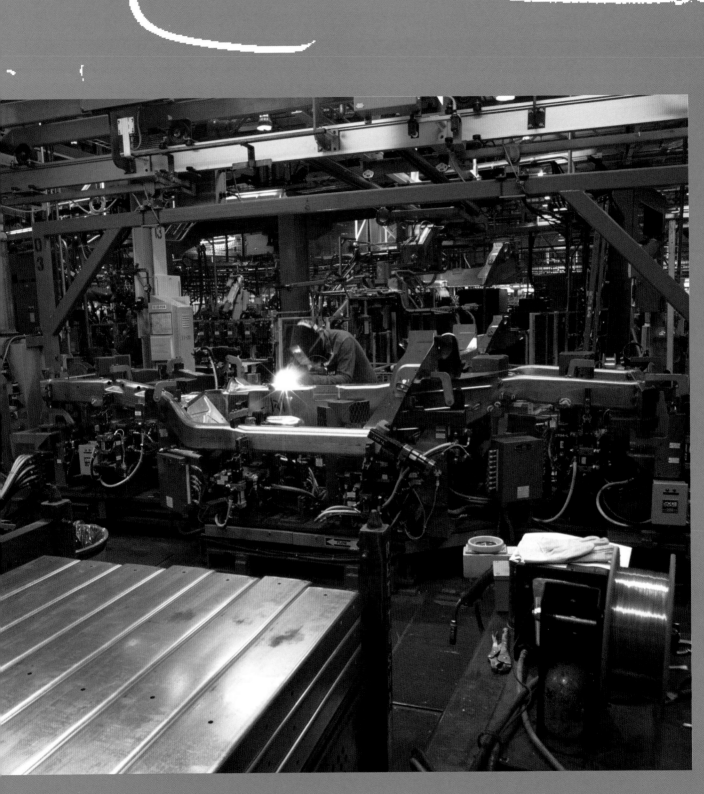

The hydroformed side rails then go to the welding shop where a workforce of robots and humans attaches the central backbone to the side rails with braces. To work in the welding shop, an employee must first go through a 40-hour precision-welding training program. *Copyright 2003 GM Corp. Used with permission, GM Media Archive*

facility lives up to its designation as an assembly plant. No parts are manufactured at Bowling Green.

It takes about three days to assemble a Corvette. Work starts by taking the 14-foot-long, hydroformed side rails, which are straight when they are shipped from the supplier, and bending them to the proper shape in a large press. The rails measure 13 feet long after the bending operation. Robotic welders then begin the process of building a C5 frame by joining a left and right side rail. Both robotic and human welders work to build the frames from 32 separate pieces — convertibles have a 33rd piece to serve as the support for the tonneau cover latch. The human welders are highly skilled in MIG welding. Meanwhile, the applicable exterior panels for each frame begin a 10-hour, 2-mile-long journey through the 250,000-square-foot paint shop.

The paint process is completely automated. In order to ensure color consistency, the paint is continually mixed in large vats instead of in separate batches. Cars painted Millennium Yellow or Anniversary Red receive six coats of paint (two primer, two color, and two clear) while all others get only a single clear coat.

The frame moves slowly along through various workstations where workers gradually add pieces and parts. Special jigs ensure that items like trunk lids, targa tops, and the Z06 hardtop all line up properly for installation. Robots apply the glue used to affix certain parts, like the hardtop, to the body. Machines move heavy items like door assemblies and window glass into position for the workers to install. Even the boxes of parts are placed on hydraulic lifts that continually keep them within easy reach of workers. This helps keep bending and lifting to a minimum.

The dash, instrument panel, windshield frame, and pedals are installed as a complete unit. The same is true for the convertible tops, which come

fully assembled from an outside supplier and arrive ready to be installed. Since cars are built in order number sequence, workers at various points are called on to perform different functions depending on whether the car coming to them will be a coupe, convertible, or hardtop. Windshields, for example, can either be the lighter weight with Head-Up Display (HUD) for a Z06; of a similar weight but either with or without HUD for convertibles; or of heavier glass with or without HUD for the coupe.

On another part of the plant floor, the suspension and drivetrain are assembled. Engines come in from the engine plant in St. Catherine, Ontario, Canada, fully assembled. They are even pre-filled with Mobil 1 synthetic oil. Bowling Green workers add the appropriate bell housing, water pump, pulleys, wiring harness, and serial number.

The front and rear suspension (including transaxle) are also assembled in this area of the plant. The complete brake system is finished here, right down to filling the master cylinder with

LEFT: To save time during the assembly process, the dash (including all instruments, controls, and wiring) as well as the steering column, pedals, and windshield are assembled off line then sent to the main line for installation. *Copyright 2003 GM Corp. Used with permission, GM Media Archive*

brake fluid. This is the only fluid that is stored within the facility. Eventually, when the cars reach the final stage of assembly, coolant, power steering fluid, and six gallons of gasoline will be added, and all of these liquids are pumped from outside storage. This filling process takes place over floor grates in case of spillage.

The completed suspension is placed on a special cart that is used to mate it with the engine and driveshaft. A worker then makes any necessary adjustments regarding the way the drive gear meshes.

Next comes the "birthing process" during which the completed body drops down from an overhead conveyor to be mated with its proper chassis moving along a line below. One worker is positioned at the rear and another at the front to line up the four main bolts that attach the body to the chassis. The rear worker

will make 10 connections, and the front worker will make 16. They guarantee that all suspension parts, hoses, and wiring is properly attached. As with all operations throughout the assembly process, specially calibrated hydraulic wrenches ensure that the proper torque is applied to all fittings.

The wheel and tire assemblies travel the greatest distance throughout the plant. They travel on an overhead conveyor that drops them down, standing right side up, onto a special installation apparatus. This tire stand floats on a cushion of air allowing the worker who handles wheel installation to quickly move it into position and easily line up the mounting holes on the wheel with the studs on the hub of the car. Once the wheel is in position, a large, round air wrench applies all five lug nuts at once.

Then, the nearly completed car slowly descends toward the touchdown point where each of the newest C5s first hits the

A special dolly is used to mate the engine with the rear-mounted transmission. At this time, the suspension and brakes are also added to the engine/transmission assembly. The master cylinder is also filled with brake fluid at this station. The entire dolly then moves along to meet up with its upper body. *Copyright 2003 GM Corp. Used with permission, GM Media Archive*

The body is lowered and "wedded" to its suspension and powertrain. A worker at the front and one at the rear line up two main bolts at either end to begin the attachment process. *Copyright 2003 GM Corp. Used with permission, GM Media Archive*

The Legend Lives
CORVETTE 5th GENERATION

CORVETTE

ground. Just before this point, the last piece is fitted to the C5. This is the black plastic bezel that surrounds the headlights.

Once on the plant floor, a new C5 is driven off the line over a short, bumpy stretch of floor. This helps settle the suspension before the car reaches the final inspection pit where alignment and other suspension settings are checked. From here, it goes to a booth where the engine, brakes, transmission, and traction control are among the various systems checked by a computer. The car sits on rollers as its driver runs it up through the gears to 70 miles per hour. The test driver swerves back and forth to check the operation of the traction control and then slams on the brakes. A green display on the monitor in the booth tells the test driver that everything is OK, and the car can be driven to the next test station. If the car fails, it goes into a nearby service bay for repairs or adjustment.

Next, the C5 heads to a booth that looks like a car wash, although its real purpose is to test for water leaks. Again, if needed, there is an area nearby where a specialist can fix any problems. There is also a body shop on the premises if more involved repairs are needed.

Finally, the new C5 sees the light of day. It is taken on a quick run over an outside test track that has a section of rough pavement. This is a final check for rattles and squeaks. Even after all this, some cars are randomly selected for quality control audits. This audit process ensures that all manufacturing tolerances and procedures are being maintained.

Cars whose new owners choose option R8C go through one additional step. They are driven over to the museum where workers specially trained by paint supplier DuPont prepare, detail, and inspect the cars for final delivery.

Even if you don't have a new car waiting at the end of the line, watching new C5s come to life is a fascinating experience. A word of warning: seeing a freshly assembled, shiny black Z06 come roaring off the assembly line can spur you to do some serious financial scheming in order to afford your own R8C delivery.

Wouldn't it be nice to see this pull into your driveway on Christmas morning? All of these cars were heading down to Florida. Note the number of 50th anniversary cars on the trailer.

chapter two
1997–1999: each year
introduces a
new flavor

PREVIOUS PAGE: During the development period, it was determined that the fifth-generation Corvette would come in three different body styles. However, only the coupe was available in 1997. The plan was for the cars to be in dealerships by the first week in January 1997, but production and quality problems weren't solved until March. Despite the delays, sales were very good. *David Newhardt*

1997: *the c5 coupe*

"Corvette is not a racing car in the accepted sense that a European car is a race car. Rather, we have built a sports car in the American tradition. It is intended to satisfy the American public's conception of beauty, plus comfort, convenience, and performance."

The preceding quote is found in the opening pages of the 1997 Corvette press kit. It'd be easy to assume that these words came right out of Dave Hill's mouth. But, actually, the statement was made by Thomas Keating, Chevrolet general manager, when he introduced the 1955 Corvette.

It would also be easy to assume that this quote is proof that the C5 was a manifestation of the theory that the more things change, the more they remain the same. But that wouldn't be correct either. As described in the first chapter, the execution of the C5 was like no other Corvette in history. The C5 may not have been intended to be a match for hardcore European road cars cum racecars—at least not until the Z06 arrived in 2001—but it was intended to be an all-American sports car that also met world-class sports car expectations.

Car "00001" rolled off the assembly line on October 1, 1996. It didn't go far. It traveled across Interstate 65 to the Corvette museum. *David Newhardt*

Unlike previous Corvettes, the C5 was designed from the start to have three models—a targa-style coupe with removable roof, a convertible, and a fixed-roof hardtop. The coupe was the first model to hit the showrooms, although not before some last-minute drama caused by production problems. The cars were intended to be delivered to dealers by January 6, 1997, the same day the C5 was unveiled to the public at the Detroit International Auto Show. However, the early run of production cars was plagued by quality problems. According to Schefter's *All Corvettes Are Red*, some of the parts that went into these cars were not up to the quality standards expected by the Corvette team. Schefter fingers the culprit as GM's policy at the time of awarding contracts to suppliers with the lowest bid. The result was that deliveries to dealers did not begin until March as Hill's people worked to iron out the wrinkles in the production system. This was the final act in the long-running melodrama of the fifth-generation Corvette.

Once it did hit the showrooms, the 1997 C5 coupe showed the world why it was worth the wait. The February 1997 issue of *Road & Track* published results of a road test of a 1997 Acura NSX-T and a separate test of the new C5. The magazine estimated the price of the NSX to be a little over $89,000 (with luxury tax estimated at $4,595). That price included ABS, dual airbags, traction control, air conditioning, stereo cassette, and a removable targa roof. The 3,090-pound, mid-engine Japanese exotic car was propelled by a 290-horsepower, 3.2-liter DOHC four-valve aluminum V-6 that rendered a zero to 60 miles per hour time of 5.0 seconds. It had an elapsed time through the quarter-mile of 13.5 seconds. Four-wheel disc brakes halted the NSX from 60 miles per hour in 123 feet. These numbers were pretty much state-of-the-art performance back in 1997 and are still very respectable today. Topping it all off was an EPA mileage estimate of 19 city/24 highway miles per gallon—not too shabby for a car with an estimated top speed of 168 miles per hour.

According to *Road & Track,* the new C5 cost about half as much as the Acura, but it was comparably equipped and included ABS, traction control, and a removable roof. Both cars had six-speed manual transmissions. The Corvette offered so much bang for the buck that *Road & Track* actually overestimated the base

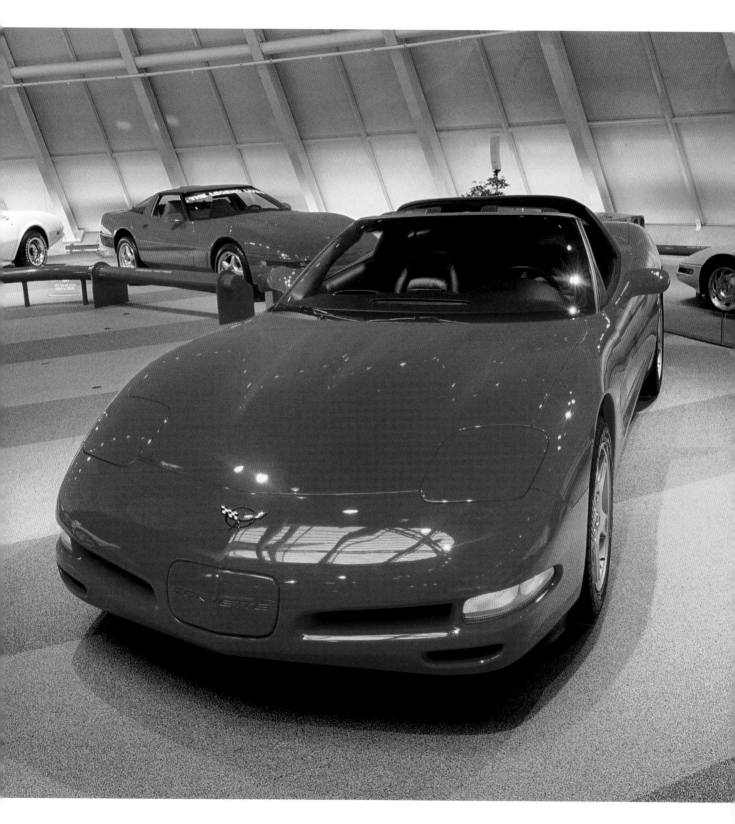

All Corvettes may not be red, but the first C5 certainly was. Here it is on display in a prominent spot at the Corvette museum in late 1996. *David Newhardt*

The cargo capacity of the C5 was nearly double that of the C4. The rear storage area had 25 cubic feet of room. Generating that much space required making Extended Mobility Tires (tires that could go 100 miles or more without air) standard equipment, thus eliminating the need for a the spare tire. Twin fuel tanks were also developed because mounting a single fuel tank in the usual location beneath the cargo floor made the storage too shallow to be of any real use. *David Newhardt*

price of the C5 coupe by $2,500. At 3,230 pounds, the C5 was slightly heavier, but with its 345-horsepower aluminum-alloy V-8, it was also more powerful. The Corvette went from zero to 60 miles per hour in 4.8 seconds and was also 0.2 seconds quicker in the quarter-mile, finishing in 13.3 seconds. Bringing it back down from 60 miles per hour to a dead stop also took less room, as the C5 could come to a halt in 116 feet. EPA fuel mileage was 18 miles per gallon in the city and an impressive 28 miles per gallon on the open road. *Road & Track* estimated its top speed to be 172 miles per hour. For any doubters who thought that the Corvette was strictly about straight-line performance, the C5 maneuvered through *R&T's* slalom course at 64.5 miles per hour, exactly 1.5 miles per hour faster than the nimble NSX.

FRAME and UNDERBODY

The C5's handling prowess was a direct result of having the stiffest body structure in Corvette history. The C5 was 4.5 times stiffer than the C4. Even with the top removed, the C5 had a higher stiffness rating than a C4 with its roof in place. This was thanks to the full-length perimeter frame with side rails made out of seamless tubular steel. The one-piece hydroformed rails were joined at either end by bumper beams that were welded, not bolted, for greater strength. The stiffer outside frame also provided for more efficient use of space inside the C5. An 8.3-inch increase in the wheelbase added only 1.2 inches in overall length compared to the C4. The doorsills were lowered by 4 inches, putting an end to the calisthenics that were required to get in and out of the C4. The rear cargo area almost doubled in usable space. There was room for two golf bags— useful for couples whose driving exercises are not confined to the road. The hydroformed frame rails also allowed the use of a "closed drivetrain tunnel" in the center of the car for additional rigidity.

The large clamshell hood of the C4 was replaced by a much simpler piece on the C5. The 5.7-liter small-block V-8 that sat under the C4's hood was also gone, replaced by a completely new V-8 with a similar 5.7-liter displacement. *David Newhardt*

Mounting the transmission at the rear of the C5 meant that the drivetrain tunnel could take up less interior space. It could avoid the wide-tapered hump that would cover the bell housing in a car with a front-mounted transmission. Additional rigidity was obtained by covering the traditionally open space below the tunnel with a bottom plate held in place by 36 bolts.

The more efficient use of space let engineers further optimize mass and stiffness by framing the C5 cockpit and windshield in a welded cage of aluminum castings and extrusions that also reduced interior vibrations. Noise and vibration were further diminished by using a cross member that provided a firm foundation for mounting the instrument panel. A magnesium steering-column support and magnesium-core steering wheel eliminated steering wheel shake while minimizing weight.

Even the floor of the C5 cockpit was re-engineered to cut down noise and vibration while increasing overall rigidity. After studying a number of alternatives, Corvette engineers came up with a combination of new-tech and old-tech materials that were 10 times stiffer than a strictly high-tech alternative. The C5 cockpit floor was basically a sandwich comprised of two layers of aerospace composite around a balsa wood core.

SUSPENSION and STEERING

The Corvette team's goal was to give the C5 world-class handling without sacrificing ride comfort. This was not an easy task considering that one is usually sacrificed to the benefit of the other, and a middle-of-the-road compromise would have certainly not been acceptable in a high-performance sports car.

The brand new suspension of the C5 featured a fully independent, four-wheel short/long-arm (SLA) setup. It incorporated forged aluminum front upper control arms and cast aluminum lower front control arms with both the rear upper and lower control arms of cast aluminum. The idea was to provide the most strength with the least mass.

A major change from the C4 was that the half shafts that transfer power from the transmission to the rear wheels no longer served as the rear suspension's upper control arms. This meant that the entire C5 suspension was mounted directly to the body to maintain the appropriate suspension geometry, providing both a smoother ride and better control.

Starting with a stiff chassis was a big advantage. This allowed the Corvette engineers to concentrate on the suspension geometry to meet their opposing goals of creating a touring car ride and providing aggressive handling. Their idea was to make the various components of the suspension complement each other in terms of compensating either for ride or handling.

For example, the extremely rigid frame allowed for the installation of lower rate (softer) springs to improve ride quality without creating a deleterious effect on road holding. While the C5 emulated the C4 with transverse composite leaf springs front and rear, the C5 springs were a new, improved design that Chevrolet patented. The springs were attached at the most rigid point of the chassis via rubber-isolated mounts for optimum control of springing forces. Each spring ran from one side of the car to the other (transversely) with spring pads located on the longer, lower control arms.

Each end of the C5 employed a different set of suspension bushings. The front bushings were quite stiff to handle the brunt of cornering forces in a stable and predictable manner. At the rear, softer bushings helped absorb the impact of bumps and other irregularities in the road surface.

To further fine-tune ride and handling, the C5 distinguished itself from the C4 by having adjustable ride height. This allowed the suspension of each C5 to be specifically calibrated at the factory to ensure proper ride and handling. The suspension was adjusted according to the car's options and equipment and their attendant weight. This feature may seem like a minor detail, but it highlights the dedication and enthusiastic attitude that spurred the Corvette team to make the C5 a world-class performer.

The 1997 C5 offered buyers a choice of three suspension setups. In addition to the base suspension were two optional suspensions—the RPO F45 Selective Real Time Damping and the RPO Z51 Performance Handling Package. The F45 allowed a driver, via a console-mounted switch, to select from three modes (Tour, Sport, and Performance) to adjust shock damping from soft to firm. Rather than simply switch between the hard and soft settings, the system was able to read the road surface at each wheel and provide a continuing range of damping adjustment accordingly. The Tour setting provided a softer ride than the base suspension, while the Performance setting approached the stiffness of the autocross-focused Z51 suspension package. Both the base and F45 suspension utilized stabilizer bars that measured 24 millimeters up front and 19.1 millimeters in the rear. The Z51, touted for weekend warriors at autocrosses and track events, included stiffer springs, larger monotube shocks, and beefier stabilizer bars that were sized at 30 millimeters for the front and 21.7 millimeters out back. Unlike that in the previous C4 iteration, the latest Z51 suspension was meant to rattle the competition at the track without rattling the fillings of C5 drivers while on the street.

The 1997 C5 came with an improved version of GM's variable effort rack-and-pinion steering system. Magnasteer II was specifically tuned for the C5 chassis to improve steering feel (the lack of which was considered to be one of the C4's major shortcomings) during cornering and high-speed transitions.

exterior

John Cafaro first became involved with Corvette design work in 1979. He admits that his love affair with the car goes back to his youth when he fell under the visual spell cast by the Mako Shark concept car. It was this heritage, plus a fascination with the flowing yet aggressive lines of Chevrolet road racing cars (like the Chaparrals and the later Corvette GTP cars) that influenced his shaping of the C5. The size and stance of the 1984 C4 and its aim to appeal to a more international audience also guided the C5's progress. But the main thing that influenced the C5's shape was the fact that an equivalent of 37 workweeks were spent in the wind tunnel.

Aerodynamics was the force that directed the honing and planing of edges and curves that chiseled the C5's silhouette down to an air friendly drag coefficient of 0.29. The tapered rear of the greenhouse and the high, squared-off rear deck with its slight trailing edge provided the proper amount of aerodynamic downforce to keep the C5 coupe glued to the road at up to 175 miles per hour.

The body panels of the C5 were not made of fiberglass. Instead, they were created from a flexible sheet-molded compound (SMC) that was more resistant to dings and dents than fiberglass was. The C5 rear quarter panels were bolted, not bonded, in place for cheaper and easier accident repairs.

The C5 driver's view was much better than that of the C4. The windshield was moved forward 7 inches, and the sloping nose allowed for a clearer view of the road. Larger exterior mirrors, brighter headlights, and an improved tandem windshield wiper system were also listed among the C5's refinements.

With 15 percent more horsepower over the base engine of the 1996 C4 (345 versus 300 horsepower), the new C5 coupe could easily dust off its predecessor. The new LS1 V-8 outmatched even the optional 330-horsepower LT4 engine of 1996. *David Newhardt*

The C5 chassis was constructed around hydroformed steel side rails, making it much stiffer with the targa top removed than its predecessor was with the roof mounted. The top was also easier to remove. It had two latches on the windshield header that did away with the special wrenches that were needed for the C4. *David Newhardt*

One final touch was the design of a new Corvette emblem to celebrate the birth of the fifth generation. The new emblem departed from the rigid, straight-edged depiction of the traditional Corvette crossed flags used on the C4 to "wave" the checkered flag along. The new version showcased the familiar all-American Chevy bow-tie logo and a fleur-de-lis to commemorate the Chevrolet brothers' French heritage.

INTERIOR

C5 buyers also got more space inside the car. Head, leg, and shoulder room were all increased along with the width of the driver's footwell. The door openings were made larger. Seat travel went up slightly. A lockable glove box returned to the dash after being absent since 1993. Cargo capacity nearly doubled to a volume of 25 cubic feet.

A passenger grab handle, reminiscent of the 1963 Sting Ray's, was added, and the ignition switch was moved back to the dash for the first time since 1968. The additional 3.1 inches in the width of the driver's footwell allowed for the placement of a "dead pedal" footrest.

A neat array of analog gauges replaced the confusing digital arcade that served as an instrument panel in the C4. The C5's instrument panel displayed a large, round tachometer and matching speedometer. They were flanked by smaller auxiliary gauges that monitored fuel level, coolant temperature, oil pressure, and voltage. A central driver information digital display was included underneath the analog gauges. The information on this display included items such as maintenance reminders, tire pressures, a trip and fuel mileage computer, and programmable settings for lighting, alarms, and seat memory. To appeal to an international audience, the display was multilingual, and drivers could choose to view the information in English, Spanish, German, or French.

The C5 entertainment system was based on a collaborative design created by Delco and Bose and used the same technology Bose had applied to the sound system of the latest Gulfstream V executive business jet.

Topping off the C5 interior was a removable top that featured a magnesium frame to make it lighter and easier to handle. A simplified latch system, which eliminated the need for special tools or wrenches, made removal and replacement a breeze.

Rear-mounted transmission

Better interior packaging and more balanced handling were two of the bonuses that resulted when the transmission was mounted at the rear of the C5. Weight distribution of the C5 was split almost equally front to rear despite the front-mounted V-8 engine. In the coupe equipped with the automatic transmission, weight distribution registered 51.4 percent in front and 48.6 percent in the rear.

The automatic transmission was a Hydra-Matic four-speed with overdrive (4L60-E). It was similar to that of the C4 but had a stiffer case and modified electronic controls. Also available as

a "no-cost" option was a Borg-Warner six-speed manual transmission. It replaced the ZF unit of the C4. The new manual transmission had a self-adjusting clutch. The transmission had the skip-shift feature that shifted from first to fourth gear under certain conditions to improve fuel economy.

The rear-mounted transmission arrangement of the C5 should not be confused with a transaxle that combines the transmission and differential in one housing. Either transmission in the C5 delivers power back to a limited-slip rear axle built by Getrag.

bigger is better

comparison of
increased interior
dimensions
1997 C5 versus 1996 C4

DIMENSION IMPROVEMENT (1997 VS. 1996)	
Head room	+1.3 inches
Leg room	+ 0.7 inches
Shoulder room	+ 1.4 inches
Driver footwell width	+ 3.1 inches
Passenger footwell width	+ 6.3 inches
Seat travel	+ 0.5 inches
Cargo capacity	+ 12.4 cubic feet
Door opening — top	+ 0.8 inches
Door opening — bottom (sill width)	- 3.7 inches

Source 1997 Corvette Press Kit

tale of the tape

C5 versus C4
specifications

The 1997 C5 matched the lowest coefficient of drag figures of any U.S. production car that year except for GM's EV-1 electric car. The long, sloping nose, courtesy of designer John Cafaro, played a major part in obtaining aerodynamic efficiency. But Dave Hill and his team still had to work hard to hit their target of 0.29. *David Newhardt*

	1996 C4 COUPE	1997 C5 COUPE
Overall length, inches	178.5	179.6
Width, inches	70.7	73.6
Height, inches	46.3	47.8
Curb weight, pounds	3,298	3,221
Wheelbase, inches	96.2	104.5
Tire Size: Front	P255/45ZR17	P245/45ZR17
Rear	P285/40ZR17	P275/40ZR18
Front track, inches	59.5	62.1
Rear track, inches	59.1	62.0

SMALL BLOCK DEVELOPS BIG POWER

the LS1 takes the iconic Chevrolet V-8 to another level

Don't let the 5.7-liter, V-8 spec of the C5 fool you. Just like the C5 chassis, the engine that powers it carries on the Corvette tradition — only this time with all-new technology and attitude. The numbers tell part of the story. The LS1 puts out 345 horsepower at 5,600 rpm. The LT4, the high-output optional engine in 1996, made 330 horsepower at 5,800 rpm. Torque also increased from 340 ft-lb at 4,500 rpm in The small-block Chevy V-8 debuted in 1955, and Ed Cole, Chevrolet's chief engineer, made sure that it was available as an option on the 1955 Corvette. Almost all of the Corvette buyers that year opted to pay the extra $235 (plus $178 for the Powerglide automatic that was a required option until late in the production year) for the 195-horsepower, 265-ci V-8 over the 155-horsepower, 235-ci inline six. As a result, in 1956 the V-8 became the Corvette's only powerplant.

For the Gen III version of the small block, which would debut exclusively in the 1997 C5, GM powertrain engineers got what many considered to be the chance of a lifetime. They were offered a clean sheet of paper to redesign the venerable small-block V-8. The LS1 5.7-liter V-8 that arrived in the C5 was technically still a pushrod V-8 of 5.7-liter capacity like the LT1 and optional LT4 of the 1996 C4, but very little was carried over from the previous year. The only dimension that remained the same was the "440 bore centers," that is, the 4.40-inch distance between bore centers that had been a trait of the small block for 40 years. "After all, some things are sacred," said John Juriga, the LS1 engine project manager.

The bore centers may have been the same, but the LS1 block departed from tradition by eschewing cast iron for aluminum with cast-iron cast-in-place cylinder liners. This historic change in materials saved 53 pounds. Comparing a complete LS1 engine to its predecessor, the total weight loss was 88 pounds.

Not only was the LS1 lighter, it was also stronger. The powertrain engineers slightly reduced the bore size with a corresponding increase in the stroke (therefore the displacement still rounded up to 5.7 liters). This provided for more room around the cylinders, which translated into a beefier, more rigid block with more room for cooling.

Another aspect of the LS1 block that made it more rigid was its overall shape. The LS1 block featured a deep skirt. Rather than end at the centerline of the crankshaft, it extended past the bearing caps. This allowed the main bearing caps to also be cross-bolted to the skirt for added strength.

New aluminum cylinder heads were held in place by four bolts, as opposed to the five that were used in the past. But because of the deep-skirt design, these bolts extended deeper into the block for less stress and distortion. The result was a better seal. Lighter-weight aluminum pistons, with the top ring moved up slightly higher to reduce emissions, enabled the LS1 to make more power at higher rpm.

The big news regarding the LS1 cylinder heads was the shape of the "replicated" ports that replaced the "siamesed" ports of the LT1 and LT4. In the LT4, the intake ports were formerly squeezed together in pairs that created variations in the flow paths. The replicated ports of the LS1 were identical. This eliminated the twists and bends that could prevent the intake air from traveling in a straight line into the cylinders. The LS1 breathed better for better performance and efficiency.

A new intake manifold rested atop the LS1. It was made of a glass-fiber-reinforced nylon composite. It was lighter than aluminum yet very durable. This new intake manifold conducted less heat than its predecessor, ensuring that incoming air was cooler, delivering a higher density, oxygen-rich charge that would make more power. The composite material made it easier to manufacture intake tubes with smooth interior walls for unobstructed air flow.

More high technology rested at the opposite end of the block. A low-profile oil sump was required for the LS1 to enable it to fit under the low hood line of the C5. Extensions sprouted from either side of the central pan, increasing oil capacity from four to six quarts. This ensured a steady supply of oil to the pickup tube to combat the high cornering forces generated by the C5 chassis. The sump's stiff construction allowed it to serve as a structural member attaching to the base of the block. This helped in reducing noise and vibration.

The LS1 also included a direct ignition system with a separate ignition coil near the spark plug of each cylinder. The traditional small block firing order was changed from 1-8-4-3-6-5-7-2 to 1-8-7-2-6-5-4-3 for added smoothness. A new-design valvetrain positioned the valves, rocker arms, and pushrods in-line to reduce the stress from side loads on these components. This, in turn, allowed for the use of lighter springs and rocker arms as well as slimmer valve stems to reduce friction and noise while also increasing the rpm limit.

Exhaust flow out of the LS1 was quickly and cleanly expelled by a true dual exhaust system. It was made of aluminized stainless steel and had dual mufflers and quad exhaust outlets. To combat cold-start emissions while improving performance, cast-iron exhaust manifolds were replaced by a dual-wall stainless steel manifold so that exhaust gasses were hotter when they reached the catalytic converters. This resulted in more effective emissions control.

Another "first" incorporated into the LS1 was the Electronic Throttle Control (ETC). It used "drive-by-wire" technology to coordinate throttle response with the traction control, cruise control, and operation of the automatic transmission. The brains of this system were provided by a multifunctional computer processor—the Powertrain Control Module (PCM). This eliminated the need for most of the engine compartment-cluttering hardware and wiring that was required by previous generation electronic control systems.

After hearing all the positive aspects of the new small block, there is one question that must be asked. Why spend all this time and energy on an ancient single-cam, pushrod engine instead of channeling it towards a more exotic double-overhead-cam, multivalve powerplant that would be more in character with the state-of-the-art, world-class aspirations of the C5?

It should come as no surprise that there indeed was some controversy in going with the pushrod engine. So, how and why was this determination made?

Tradition was one factor in the decision to go with the pushrod technology. Chevrolet had been burned by the four-cam, 32-valve LT5 that was the heart of the ZR-1 Corvette. The complex engine, developed with Lotus and built by Mercury Marine, was an expensive experiment that lost its consumer appeal by the time it finally reached its full potential. It also nearly doubled the price of a Corvette so equipped. Remember, a big part of getting management approval for the C5 was being able to convince management that a market existed for such a car during a downturn in the economy.

In the end, the company decided to go with a pushrod engine because it could be made to fit under the low hood of the C5. And, based on advances the powertrain engineers built into the LS1, that proved to be a wise choice.

SMALL BLOCK V-8 COMPARISON

	1996 LT1 (BASE C4)	1996 LT4 (OPT. C4)	1997 LS1
DISPLACEMENT	5.7 liters	5.7 liters	5.7 liters
BORE X STROKE (INCHES)	4.00 x 3.48	4.00 x 3.48	3.90 x 3.62
HORSEPOWER (SAE NET)	300 at 5,000 rpm	330 at 5,800 rpm	345 at 5,600 rpm
TORQUE (FT-LB)	335 at 3,600 rpm	340 at 4,500 rpm	350 at 4,400 rpm
EPA MILEAGE – AUTO.	17/25 city/hwy.	N/A	17/25 city/hwy.
EPA MILEAGE – MAN.	N/A	16/27 city/hwy.	18/28 city hwy.

UNDER PRESSURE: C5 TIRE CHOICE

The C5 was the first Corvette to have staggered tires and wheels. The front tires were 17 inches in diameter riding on 8.5-inch wheels, while the rears were 18-inchers on 9.5-inch wheels.

The C5 was also the first Corvette to delete the spare tire from the standard equipment list. Goodyear Eagle F1 GS Extended Mobility Tires (EMTs) were developed for the C5 with reinforced sidewalls that could support the weight of the car in case of a loss of air pressure. These run-flat tires could be driven without air at speeds up to 55 miles per hour for at least 100 miles. They allowed the spare tire and the tire-changing tools that accompanied it to be eliminated. By eliminating the spare and the jack, the Corvette team was able to decrease the car's weight. This resulted in both improved mileage and performance as well as more usable cargo space. From an ergonomics perspective, the area where the spare tire would have to be mounted (at the rear of the cargo area) would have seriously hindered outside accessibility to the cargo area. What Chevrolet refers to as the "trunk area reach-over distance" was reduced by nearly 14 inches. This made it easier for owners to get their golf bags into the trunk and helped save the finish on the rear fenders.

Run-flat tires were an option on the C4 since the 1994 model year. More than a quarter of all Corvette buyers selected this option on the C4. Market research indicated that the reason buyers chose this option was not for extra luggage space or to save weight, but instead to avoid the hassle of wrestling with a large, dirty wheel and an unusable flat tire.

Despite all of the positive reasons listed above, the decision to do away with the spare tire was made only after a great deal of discussion. The sales side, led by Chevrolet general manager Jim Perkins, had opposed the idea. Additionally, during the C5's early development stages, a few states still had laws on the books requiring all cars to be equipped with spare tires. GM lobbyists took care of the latter problem while the results of research clinics proved to the sales people that Corvette buyers overwhelmingly approved the concept of not having to deal with changing a spare tire.

The EMTs worked so well that the C5 was equipped with a tire-pressure monitoring system to help the average driver tell if he actually had a flat. The system, which operated at speeds above 15 miles per hour, used battery-powered sensors inside each valve stem to transmit, via an FM radio signal, pressure readings to the Driver Information Center display on the instrument panel. GM claimed the sensors provided accurate readings within 1 psi with compensation for altitude.

While both engineering and design were in agreement over the use of run-flat tires, there was some disagreement regarding tire sizing. From a styling standpoint, John Cafaro favored a staggered setup that utilized wide tires as large as 19 inches in the rear. From both an aerodynamic and weight-saving perspective, Hill's engineers preferred to go with the narrowest 17-inch tires possible. Part of the reason was that larger tires create more drag. While reaching a Coefficient of drag of 0.30 in the wind tunnel had been relatively easy, getting down to Hill's target of 0.29 could only be attained through a trial-and-error process of niggling adjustments to the exterior before finally being achieved by streamlining the C5's undersides. Saving weight was also paramount if the C5 was to avoid the federal "gas-guzzler tax" and get in a more favorable weight class for the calculation of EPA ratings.

The issue of whether to use the larger rear tires was settled when Joe Spielman inspected a full-sized C5 clay model with the staggered setup on one side and a set of 17s on the other. Upon circling the model, Spielman decreed that the car did not look aggressive enough with the smaller rear tires. That settled the issue. Hill did win one minor battle in the tire war. He had Goodyear develop a slightly narrower tire than that used on the C4 and made sure it was done without compromising the tire's cornering capabilities.

The cornering power of the C5 comes from a sophisticated aluminum independent front and rear suspension with composite transverse leaf springs and anti-roll bars at either end. The C5 was also the first Corvette to feature a staggered wheel arrangement with 17-inch tires and wheels up front and more aggressive looking 18-inch tires and wheels at the rear. *David Newhardt*

1998: the C5 convertible debuts

The debut of the all-new, fifth-generation Corvette coupe may have elevated the pulse rates of automotive enthusiasts and the media, but Corvette fever reached epidemic proportions when the C5 convertible hit the street. Chevrolet arranged for a caravan of 20 new Corvette convertibles to spend two weeks in September 1997 cruising from Chicago to California on Route 66. America's most historic highway was the perfect place to introduce the latest Corvette convertible to the public.

The 1998 convertible was 114 pounds lighter than the 1996 C4 convertible it succeeded. And with a base price of $44,425, it was $635 cheaper. The price differential was even higher after taking into account that the C5 ragtop included about $1,500 of additional standard equipment such as speed-sensitive steering, run-flat tires, a higher-quality Bose stereo system, and power driver's seat.

And, for the first time since 1962, the C5 convertible had a real trunk. This gave the C5 convertible twice the cargo volume (13.9 cubic feet) of a C4 convertible when the top was up—and four times as much storage space (11.1 cubic feet) when the top was down. These figures were also higher than those tallied by competitors such as the Porsche 911 Carrera Cabriolet, the BMW Z3, and, of course, the cramped Dodge Viper RT/10.

The biggest advantage that the C5 had over its immediate predecessor was that it was designed to be a convertible from the ground up. The torsional rigidity of the C5 convertible, according to Chevrolet engineers, was only about 10 percent less than a C5 coupe with its top in place. Vibration frequency is a test of a chassis' rigidity, and it indicates how well the chassis responds to irregularities in the road surface. Engineers measure it by a hertz rating of vibration cycles per second—the higher the hertz rating, the better. The C5 coupe measured a high of 27 hertz, while a C5 convertible recorded only slightly less at 23 hertz. These numbers compared quite favorably to the 1997 Mercedes-Benz SL 500, which was, at the time, considered to a be a rock-steady roadster. It measured an 18 hertz rating.

An illustration of 1998 C5 convertible shows how the wide doorsills of the C4 were eliminated by the hydroformed perimeter rail frame. The frame also added much-needed stiffness. It also had the first real trunk on a Corvette convertible since the 1962 model year. Cargo capacity was double that of the C4 convertible with the top up—and four times as great with the top lowered. *Copyright 2003 GM Corp. Used with permission, GM Media Archive*

Despite the fabric top and the coupe's more aerodynamic tapered rear window, the C5 convertible still managed an aero-friendly drag coefficient of 0.33. This number was almost identical to that posted by the Acura NSX-T targa-style coupe, the production sports car with the next best coefficient of drag. *Copyright 2003 GM Corp. Used with permission, GM Media Archive*

The rigidity of the C5 convertible was even more impressive when you take into consideration that it only weighed a pound more than the coupe. The same weight-saving ideals that applied to the coupe were in effect for the convertible. That is why a manually operated top was chosen. The idea was to save weight and to take up less storage space.

The top showcases what GM calls a pressurized, five-bow design. It only required loosening two latches on the windshield

To save weight, a manual top was used on the C5 convertible. The top folded easily out of sight below the tonneau panel behind the seats. Two latches fastened the top to the windshield header, one button raised the tonneau cover, and tension forced the fifth bow into providing a secure, leakproof seal without snaps or latches. Dave Hill said the top was tested at speeds up to 170 miles per hour. *Copyright 2003 GM Corp. Used with permission, GM Media Archive*

Designed as a convertible from the ground up, the C5 convertible was only about 10 percent less rigid than the C5 coupe with its targa top in place. The new convertible was also 114 pounds lighter than its C4 counterpart, and its base price was $635 less with a longer standard equipment list. *Copyright 2003 GM Corp. Used with permission, GM Media Archive*

header and then folding both ends up toward the middle. A button released the tonneau cover behind the seats, allowing the top to be stowed beneath it. Raising the top was just as easy. The pressurized construction referred to the tension created when the top was fully opened. This forced the rear top bow down into position on the rear deck to create a weatherproof seal without the need for locating pins or snaps.

The coefficient of drag of the convertible, 0.33, was only slightly higher than that of the coupe. Headroom was only decreased by 1/4 inch. Hill claimed that the top had been tested at speeds up to 170 miles per hour without any negative effects.

Not only did the Corvette convertible return to the streets in 1998, it returned to the races as a pace car. It was outfitted with a required roll bar and strobe warning lights behind each seat and had a Radar Blue (but purple-looking) paint job, yellow wheels, and an eye-searing yellow stripe/graphics package. The 1998 C5 convertible became the fourth Corvette and eleventh Chevrolet to pace the Indianapolis 500. Jon Moss, GM manager of special vehicles, was the man whose job it was to build the pace cars in addition to some wild in-house hot rods. He reported that, because of the Corvette team's diligent work in developing the C5 chassis and potent LS1 engine, not much work was required beyond the paint job to get the vehicle in pace car shape. The only hiccup in the process was that, after a media blitz touting golfer Greg Norman as the designated driver, a shoulder injury put the "Shark" on the shelf just prior to the 500. The car appropriately wound up in the hands of 1963 Indy winner Parnelli Jones.

Chevrolet built 1,163 Indy Pace Car Replica (RPOZ4Z) convertibles that emulated the color scheme and graphics of the original. Of these, 616 were equipped with automatic transmissions. For the $5,039 option, all the replicas could be considered fully equipped, minus a 12-disc CD changer and magnesium wheels that were separate options.

Not only did the pace car replicas have almost everything you could buy from the 1998 option list, they also had something that would not be available on other Corvettes until later in the model year. Included with the Z4Z package was the Active Handling System that would soon become a separate option (RPO JL4). This was essentially a stability package that worked in conjunction with the ABS and Traction Control. Active Handling sensors monitored the yaw rate (the vehicle's rotation), steering angle (driver input), lateral acceleration, and brake pressure. If the system sensed that either the front (understeer)

Parnelli Jones, shown here signing a model of the 1998 C5 Indy pace car that he drove, was a last-minute substitute for golfer Greg Norman. Besides winning the 500 in 1963, P.J. had also driven a Ford Mustang as the pace car in 1994. He remembers the Corvette as being a "fun car to drive, but I wasn't crazy about the color." He also remembers that Ford gave him the Mustang after the race while Chevrolet did not follow suit.

or rear (oversteer) end of the car was losing traction, it applied brake pressure to one or more wheels as needed to assist the driver in regaining control.

A unique feature of the Corvette's Active Handling was that, besides the ability to be switched off with a quick push of the console-mounted button, it also offered the driver a third option—Competition Mode. With the engine running and the vehicle stopped, depressing the Active Handling "off" switch for five seconds activated Competition Mode. In Competition Mode, designed for track use, only Traction Control was turned off while ABS and Active Handling remained active. The latter was another sign that the driving enthusiasts on the inside of GM were looking out for the needs of driving enthusiasts on the outside of the corporate walls.

1999: *the hardtop*

The third version of the C5, the hardtop, debuted in 1999, but it was not quite the Billy Bob special that Jim Perkins had envisioned. At a base price of $38,777, the hardtop was the cheapest Corvette available—$394 less than the nearest priced model. It did lack some items that were standard on the coupe and convertible, notably a power driver's seat and upgraded stereo sys-

tem, but it was not the low-ball-priced "stripper" that Perkins and others thought would be needed to boost sales to the necessary 25,000 per year they guaranteed upper management when arguing the case for the C5.

"At one time," recalls Tadge Juechter, "that cheap car was going to have a smaller engine, a 4.8- or 5.2-liter. This was

In 1999, the hardtop model made its debut, and the Corvette C5 family was complete. Originally intended to be a bare-bones model nicknamed "Billy Bob," the hardtop was the lowest priced C5 model and went without some of the options available on the coupe and convertible including automatic transmission. *Copyright 2003 GM Corp. Used with permission, GM Media Archive*

A new option for 1999 was the Head-Up Display (HUD) that projected various instrument readouts onto the windshield to allow a driver to focus on the road and not the instrument panel. The driver had a choice of which instruments to display including the speedometer, tachometer, fuel level, water temperature, and oil pressure. *Copyright 2003 GM Corp. Used with permission, GM Media Archive*

dropped at the very last minute, but some of the pilot cars had already been built. These had smaller tires and wheels, automatic transmission, manual mirrors—a real strippo. Meanwhile, the 1997 and 1998 were selling like hotcakes."

In less than a half-year of sales, Corvette sold 9,752 coupes. In 1998, 19,235 coupes rolled out of the Bowling Green facility along with 11,849 convertibles for a total of 31,084 cars. The C5 was a hit. Sales in 1999 added up to 33,270 cars including 4,031 hardtops.

Market clinics confirmed that Corvette owners felt that selling a watered-down coupe to reach a $32,000 price would cheapen the car's image and anger those who were willing to spend more to get something that lived up to the Corvette image.

"At the very last minute we said, 'OK, we'll make this a high performance model with only a manual transmission and the Z51 suspension on it,'" Juechter says. "It was slightly faster, but not by much."

The performance advantage of the hardtop stemmed from the fact that it was slightly stiffer and slightly lighter than the coupe. Hill came up with the idea of gluing and bolting a hardtop onto the existing convertible chassis, and the addition of the top structurally strengthened an already rigid, albeit open, chassis. At a

The C5 hardtop also made its debut on the racetrack in 1999, serving as a pace car at the Daytona 24 Hours race in January. Already equipped with the Z51 suspension and a six-speed manual transmission, the only work required by Jon Moss of GM Special Vehicles was to add chrome wheels, graphics, a sporty exhaust, and the necessary strobe warning lights. *Copyright 2003 GM Corp. Used with permission, GM Media Archive*

curb weight of 3,174 pounds, the hardtop was 56 pounds lighter than a coupe. The hardtop did create a bit more aerodynamic drag than the coupe with a coefficient of drag of 0.31. It also had the least amount of storage space—13.3 cubic feet—despite sharing the trunk from the convertible.

The hardtop was only available with the six-speed manual transmission and the Z51 suspension. It also had a shorter option list than the coupe or convertible, notably lacking luxury accessories such as dual-zone air conditioning, the Memory Package, power passenger seat, Sport Seats, a power telescoping steering wheel, Twilight Sentinel, and the Head-Up Display instrument package.

The last three items, by the way, were new additions to the Corvette coupe and convertible option list in 1999. The Head-Up Display (HUD) projected vehicle speed, engine rpm, and other driver selectable information onto the windshield allowing the driver to monitor these functions without taking his eyes off the road.

Twilight Sentinel used a low-light sensor to automatically turn on the headlights. For added nighttime security, it also featured a delay in dousing the headlights after the ignition had been switched off. The power telescoping steering wheel had a 20-millimeter range of adjustment. Tilt remained a manual adjustment.

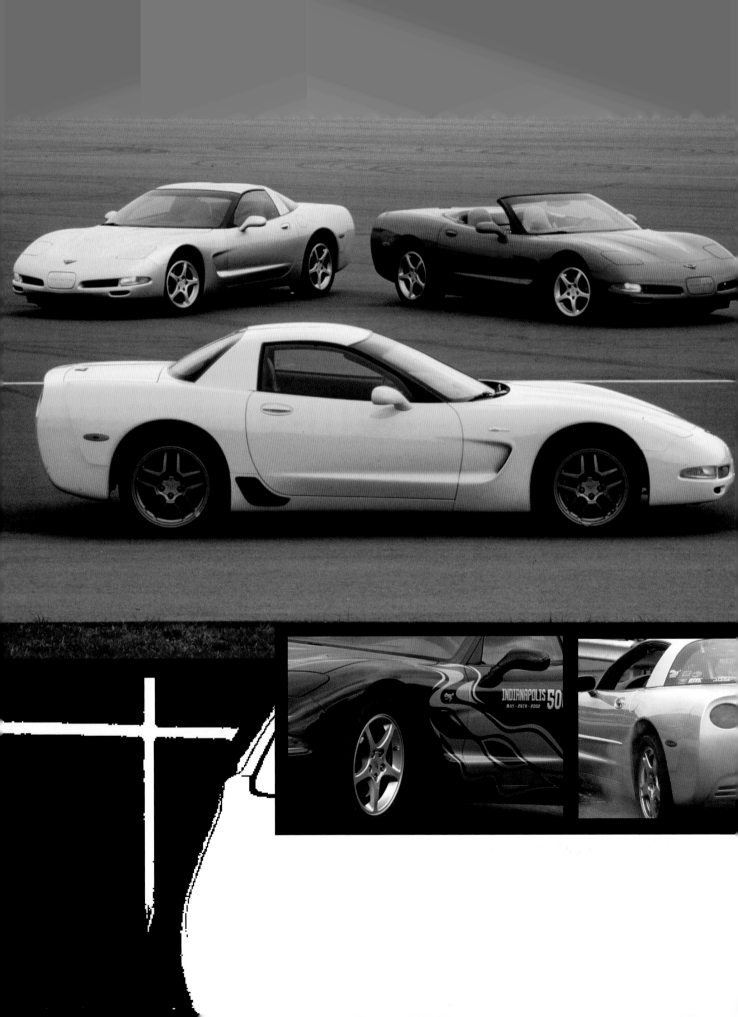

CHAPTER THREE
2000-2004: the C5 keeps getting better

"The first three years [were] Boom-Boom-Boom," says Tadge Juechter about bringing the C5 to the market. "We really pushed ourselves, so in 2000 we took a little breather, although nobody really liked the wheels we had from 1997, so we brought out the high-polished forged wheels."

Spoken just like a true enthusiast. Even when the members of the Corvette team seemed to be resting, their minds were still working on ways to make improvements. Besides addressing the new five-spoke, forged-aluminum wheels, they also made revisions to the Z51 suspension in the form of beefier front and rear stabilizer bars and revalved shock absorbers. The LS1 emissions were tidied up to cut nitrogen oxide by 50 percent and hydrocarbons by 70 percent to meet the Low Emission Vehicle (LEV) standard.

Passive Keyless Entry (PKE) was locked away into Corvette history. It was replaced by the much simpler to use Active Keyless Entry. Also disappearing with PKE was the passenger door lock cylinder.

2001

The transformation of the hardtop into the modern iteration of the Z06 captured most of the attention in the 2001 model year. The Z06 eliminated 130 pounds and added 30 horsepower (resulting in a total of 385 horsepower) to become the weapon of choice for the weekend warriors who wanted a Corvette that they could drive on the track as well as to work. In addition to its more powerful LS6 version of the small-block V-8, bigger brakes, a more aggressive suspension setup, and larger wheels and tires were also part of the Z06 equipment list. To please buyers looking for something sporty, but a little less over the top, the 2001 coupe and convertible models also underwent changes to make them a bit more powerful and agile as well as more refined. To quote Dave Hill, "We've expanded the envelope in every direction."

The LS1 got a revised intake manifold with increased plenum volume and smoother flowing intake runners. Forcing more air

A revised intake manifold increased air flow into the 2001 LS1 allowing it to make 350 horsepower at 5,600 rpm. Torque also increased to 360 ft-lb at 4,400 rpm on cars equipped with automatic transmissions (about 60 percent of C5s sold). This boosted initial throttle response on these cars as well as lowering the zero to 60 acceleration time to 5.0 seconds flat.

into the engine increased horsepower to 350 at 5,600 rpm. The increased volume of air allowed engineers to adjust camshaft lift and overlap to improve the torque curve. Torque went up from 350 to 360 ft-lb at 4,400 rpm on automatic transmission models and to 375 ft-lb on the manual transmission cars. This translated to a crisper initial throttle response, especially in the cars with automatic transmissions—about 60 percent of C5s. Acceleration times from zero to 60 miles per hour were listed as 5.0 seconds for the automatic and 4.5 seconds for the manual transmission.

Stick shift drivers were not forgotten when it came to the 2001 improvement list. The clutch was made stronger to handle the torque increase, yet pedal effort was reduced for easier engagement.

A second generation of Active Handling became standard equipment. The system boasted hardware (Bosch 5.3 hydraulic pressure modulator) and software (sideslip angle rate control, dynamic rear brake proportioning, rear brake stability control) improvements to become less intrusive, improve response time in cold weather, and be better coordinated with traction control. To engage the Competition Mode, it was no longer necessary to bring the vehicle to a complete stop.

In terms of refinement, 2001 Corvettes benefited from improved sound insulation and seals, the addition of chrome finish to the exhaust tips, and an Absorbent Glass Mat (AGM) battery. The new-technology battery used fiberglass mats impregnated with electrolyte that was compressed along with the lead plates into a sealed, reinforced case. The new battery weighed 5.7 pounds less than its predecessor, was more heat resistant, and could be recharged more often than a lead-acid battery.

Convertibles got new tops that had better insulation, a better seal, and a smoother appearance.

2002

The noise coming out of the Corvette camp in 2002 was the growl of more horsepower for the Z06 LS6 engine. That was followed by the applause of car enthusiasts. There were some appealing sounds for coupe and convertible buyers, too, in the form of the AM/FM stereo with in-dash CD player, which became standard equipment. The AM/FM/cassette player was only available with the 12-disc CD changer.

If you were one of the lucky ones at Indy in 2002, you got a rather plain, but very important, limited edition ticket to experience a ride around the oval in the C5 pace car. A commemorative model, packed inside a box featuring a backdrop portrait of the famed "Brickyard," was included in the deal.

For the second time in its history, the C5 Corvette was chosen to pace the Indy 500 in 2002. Both the color scheme and the driver were less colorful than those in 1998. Anniversary Red replaced Radar Blue, while actor Jim Caviezel played the role of pace car driver. *Copyright 2003 GM Corp. Used with permission, GM Media Archive*

Chevrolet has been chosen 13 times to pace the Indianapolis 500. Of those, a Corvette has represented the marque on five occasions. Here is a family reunion of all the Corvette pace cars. The cars are from 1978, 1986, 1995, 1998 and 2002 (actually a 2003 model). *Copyright 2003 GM Corp. Used with permission, GM Media Archive*

Jumping the gun by a year or so, a special 50th anniversary edition of the C5 became the fifth Corvette (and second C5) selected to pace the Indianapolis 500, on May 26, 2002. Similar to the 50th anniversary coupe that would go on sale later in the year as a 2003 model, the pace car had special exterior graphics applied to an Anniversary Red exterior and a lower restriction muffler system. Requirements for use at the Speedway included the installation of four-point, racing-type safety belts and a safety strobe light system. Also added were heavy-duty transmission and steering coolers to ensure optimum performance while leading a pack of Indy Cars around the historic oval.

2003

In honor of the Corvette's 50th birthday, the C5 was released in 50th Anniversary Special Edition coupe and convertible models. These cars featured Anniversary Red exterior paint, specific anniversary badges, Shale leather interior, and champagne-painted anniversary wheels with special emblems. Also included in the anniversary edition package were embroidered badges on the seats and floor mats along with padded door armrests and grips. The convertible sported a Shale-colored top.

In addition to the aesthetic goodies, the special-edition cars also featured the latest in Corvette technology in the form of Magnetic Selective Ride Control. Optional on all other Corvettes for 2003, Magnetic Selective Ride Control employed a new form of shock-absorber design filled with Magneto-Rheological (MR) fluid. By controlling the current to an electromagnetic coil inside the piston of the shock absorber, the MR fluid's consistency could be changed, resulting in continuously variable real-time damping. The object was to give drivers a quieter, flatter ride as well as precise, responsive handling—particularly during sudden, high-speed maneuvers. The system worked with traction control on slippery or rough roads to assure maximum stability. It also teamed with ABS to assure balance and control.

The pace car previewd the color scheme chosen by Chevrolet to celebrate the Corvette's 50th anniversary with a run of special Anniversary Edition coupes and convertibles in 2003. *Copyright 2003 GM Corp. Used with permission, GM Media Archive*

A host of new standard equipment was added to the coupe and convertible models for 2003, including fog lamps, sport seats, a power passenger seat, dual-zone automatic climate control, and a parcel net and luggage shade on the coupe. The 2003 Corvette also included CRAS child seat hooks on the passenger seat to be used with the airbag-off switch to disable the passenger-side airbag when using a child seat.

Last but not least, all 2003 Corvettes got a party favor in the form of a special 50th anniversary emblem on the front and rear. The silver emblem displays the number 50 with the Corvette signature cross-flag design.

The special logo designed for the Corvette's 50th anniversary includes a large number 50 with the traditional crossed flags. One flag is checkered, while the other bears a Chevy bow-tie emblem along with a *fleur-de-lis* representing the French heritage of the brothers Chevrolet. *Copyright 2003 GM Corp. Used with permission, GM Media Archive*

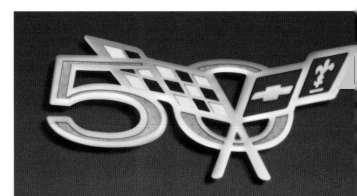

Shale leather seats bearing embroidered 50th anniversary logos are part of the special Anniversary Edition interior package that also includes floor mats with anniversary logos and color-coordinated leather door pulls and armrest pads. The shale leather interior was exclusive to the Anniversary Edition.

Anniversary Red paint and a prominent logo on the hood may not be traffic stoppers, but they do make the 50th anniversary Corvette stand out from its siblings.

The Anniversary Edition Coupe had a base price of $49,435, while the convertible started at $56,335. Both versions had the same interior and exterior color scheme; the convertible added a Shale top.

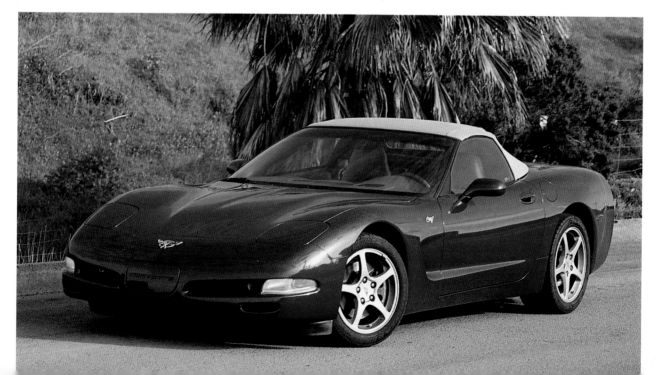

Champagne-colored, five-spoke aluminum wheels were only available on the Anniversary Edition. Although considered a bit conservative by many, in the right lighting the metallic red paint and champagne wheels are a striking combination. Dave Hill says "the paint job lights up your life on a sunny day."

The Anniversary Edition is special for what you can't see as well as what you can. Magnetic Selective Ride Control, an option on other 2003 coupe and convertible models, was standard equipment. The system allows a driver to "dial in" ride comfort or precise, flatter handling. A console-mounted switch activates the system and provides electromagnetic control over each shock absorber's damping action. Dave Hill feels that the Anniversary Edition Corvette with Magnetic Selective Ride Control is the perfect Corvette for daily driving.

The irony of the C5 50th Anniversary Edition is that if everything had gone according to plan, the C5 would have debuted in 1993 as the 40th Anniversary Edition. Maybe that's why the exterior paint is so similar to that year's Ruby Red anniversary paint job.

Notice anything unusual about this 2003 C5 other than its gold paint job? It is the world's only coupe with ZO6 rear brake cooling ducts. The coupe, which also sports gold brake calipers and gold accent stripes, is a one-off designed and created as part of the assembly plant's "Going For The Gold" drive to win the JD Power Gold award given to North America's best assembly plant. In 2002, the plant earned a Silver award. The gold C5 was raffled off to raise funds for the National Corvette Museum. Ticket sales for the raffle were limited to 2,003 entries and were sold for $200 each. The inner structure of the car has been autographed by the people who assembled it.

2004

The final year of C5 production featured Commemorative Edition coupes and convertibles (RPO Z15) plus a Commemorative Edition Z06 (RPO Z16).

The C5 Commemorative Edition models featured a Le Mans Blue exterior finish, Shale interior, special badges, special seat embroidery, and high-polish, five-spoke aluminum wheels with special center caps. The convertible model had a Shale top.

A trio of 2004 C5 models arrive at the National Corvette Museum as part of the festivities during the April 2003 C5 Birthday Bash celebration. Paying tribute to the new color scheme worn by the C5-Rs at Le Mans in 2003, the 2004 Commemorative Edition models featured a Le Mans Blue exterior finish, Shale interior, special badges, special seat embroidery, and high-polish, five-spoke aluminum wheels with special center caps. The convertible model had a Shale top. *National Corvette Museum*

ABOVE: Smoke 'em if you got 'em! Drag racing, autocrossing, road tours, and special guests like the C5-R racing team and Dave Hill were part of the four-day C5 Birthday Bash celebration that took place in April 2003. The Corvette museum and the C5 Registry owners group coordinate the annual event. *National Corvette Museum*

Just as Cobra owners love to have Carroll Shelby's autograph on everything they own, Corvette enthusiasts like to show their appreciation for Dave Hill's contribution to Corvette history. Many Corvette drivers feel that the opportunity to meet other owners as well as members of the Corvette team at events like the Birthday Bash is an important part of the Corvette ownership experience. *National Corvette Museum*

CHAPTER FOUR

LESS is MORE—
the ZO6 REVIVAL

PREVIOUS PAGE: Subtle styling touches like mesh-covered ducts in front fascia and ahead of the rear wheels serve a functional purpose while visually separating the Z06 from less potent C5s. The Z06 wheels not only feature a unique design but are also 1 inch wider front and rear than those on the coupes or convertibles. EMT tires are also discarded in favor of high-performance rubber and a can of flat tire sealant.

What happens when performance fanatics set out to build a budget version of America's sports car? When the tire smoke clears what emerges is the fastest, best-handling, most fun-to-drive regular production Corvette ever.

The Z06 model that bellowed into the 2001 Corvette lineup was originally intended to be an inexpensive, no-frills version. But once Dave Hill and his crew got the car stripped down to lean, they just couldn't resist making it mean. Fortunately, this temptation arose during a period when the automotive marketplace was breaking all previous sales records. The timing allowed a window of opportunity through which the Corvette team could drive a decontented 385-horsepower version of the Corvette that qualified as a bargain hunter deal as well as a trophy hunter special.

One of the major factors contributing to the tardy arrival, and even threatening the very existence of the C5, was the huge financial hit General Motors had taken during the recession of the late 1980s and early 1990s. When the C5 did finally emerge in 1997, management was still wary about the marketability of its low-volume, high-dollar sports car should the financial situation turn ugly again. Company sales forecasts took a conservative approach in predicting that the sales boom that started in the mid-1990s could not last into the next millennium. That's what prompted the directive for Hill to start working on a wallet-friendly version of the C5. Fortunately for all, especially those who get to spend seat time in a Z06, GM's gloomy forecast proved to be way off base, opening the door for those who wanted to make the Z06 more like its Zora Arkus-Duntov-designed namesake.

The original Z06 also owed its conception to a corporate mandate, but true to Arkus-Duntov's competitive attitude and his rebellious nature, it was designed to circumvent GM's adherence

The Z06 name recalls one of the shorter, but more interesting, pages of Corvette racing history. In order to circumvent GM's factory racing ban, in 1962 Zora Arkus-Duntov came up with the Z06 option package for the new Sting Ray. It was essentially a road racer special designed to take on Ford and its alliance with Carroll Shelby's Cobras. The car shown here is one of the original four cars commissioned by Zora. It was first campaigned by Bob Bondurant. Bondurant's sponsor was Washburn Chevrolet in Santa Barbara. The dealer was located at 614 Chapala Street, hence the number on his car. *Bob Bondurant Collection*

to the Automobile Manufacturers Association's ban on racing activity. In addition to his notable technical savvy, Arkus-Duntov was also a respected race driver, having raced for both the Allard and Porsche teams at Le Mans in the early 1950s. He had cut his teeth racing sports cars, and the idea that a corporate policy could derail him from putting a competitive Corvette on the track had him gnashing his teeth. In 1962, the knowledge that Ford and Carroll Shelby were teaming up to unleash the Cobra in international road racing competition increased his frustration. With the introduction of the 1963 Sting Ray, Arkus-Duntov felt he had a road course-worthy Corvette thanks to its new independent rear suspension. He was determined to assemble a competition package that would make use of the improved handling of the new rear setup to take on the Cobra. He may have been forbidden to create a factory race team, but no one was about to stop him from offering private entrants a special competition option that included factory-designed road-racing pieces. If you were a prospective Corvette racer, you merely had to stop by your local Chevy dealer where you could check off the Z06 RPO (Regular Production Option) on the order form. That got you Arkus-Duntov-derived goodies such as Al-fin power drum brakes with sintered metallic linings (four-wheel discs didn't debut until 1965), heavy-duty front and rear stabilizer bars, beefier shocks and springs, a dual master brake cylinder, and an endurance-racing 36.5-gallon fuel tank. Of course, you also had to have $4,257.00 for a base-model 1963 "split-window" Sting Ray coupe plus the $1,818.45 cost of the Z06 package and another $661.75 for mandatory options like the L84 360-horsepower, fuel-injected version of the 327 V-8 ($430.40), four-speed manual transmission ($188.03), and the immortal

The latest version of the Z06 arrived in 2001 as an extension of the enthusiast-oriented hardtop C5 envisioned by former Chevrolet general manager Jim Perkins. A small group of dedicated motor heads within the Corvette ranks was less than content with the budget-conscious nature of the 1999 hardtop. The group set out to take the lightest of the C5 models and build a car that weekend warriors could race on Sunday and take to work on Monday. *Copyright 2003 GM Corp. Used with permission, GM Media Archive*

Positraction rear axle ($43.05). Just like today, speed cost money. But the go-fast parts cost proportionately more in the original Z06 than they do in the contemporary model. With the cost of these required "options" bundled into the Z06 package price tag, the grand total of $2,480.20 came to 58 percent of what the bare-bones coupe itself cost. To prove that the Z06 was aimed at weekend warriors, a team of

Redheaded and red-blooded, the LS6 V-8 is the heart of the Z06 package. Like the Z06, it also recalls a potent name from the past. The original LS6 engine was a 454-ci monster with aluminum heads that put out 425 horsepower. The LS6 that appeared in 2001 was lighter and about 100-ci smaller, but it still managed to put out 385 horsepower. *Copyright 2003 GM Corp. Used with permission, GM Media Archive*

In 2002, Corvette engineers upped the ante—and the horsepower—pushing the LS6 to 405 horsepower at 6,000 rpm. Titanium exhaust, lighter wheels, and even lighter-weight window glass are all things that the Corvette team has utilized to shave weight off the Z06. The 2003 model shown here is virtually identical to the 2002. *Copyright 2003 GM Corp. Used with permission, GM Media Archive*

cars was driven directly from the St. Louis factory to California for a three-hour endurance race at Riverside Raceway on October 13, 1962. Bob Bondurant, Dave McDonald, and Jerry Grant did the driving on the road and at the track. A fourth car belonging to Mickey Thompson had been air freighted to California earlier. It was raced by Doug Hooper.

The race was especially important because it marked the competition debut of the Cobra. Although it led early, mechanical problems ended the Shelby car's race, and the Z06 of Mickey Thompson and Doug Hooper went on to win. Despite that auspicious beginning, only 199 Z06 Sting Ray coupes were built. A cheaper version of the Z06 option ($1,293.95 excluding knock-off wheels and the large-capacity fuel tank) for convertible buyers

also became available later in the 1963 model year. Dick Guldstrand raced a Z06-equipped convertible for much of 1963 until a rear wheel fell off causing a violent high-speed crash that destroyed the car.

Forty years later, the new Z06 proved a worthy successor. It could send shivers up the spine of middle-aged Cobras as well as new Ferraris, Porsches, and other world-class sports cars with price tags at least double that of the Corvette. Like its ancestor, the latest Z06 was targeted to the weekend warriors who compete at autocrosses and track events on Sunday, but need a car they can drive to work on Monday. Dave Hill reports that the historic RPO number was plucked out of the archives at the suggestion of Bill Nichols. According to Hill, when Nichols

At 3,118 pounds, the 2003 Z06 is 128 pounds lighter than the curb weight of a coupe. The convertible is only 2 pounds heavier than a coupe. Not only are there differences in the weight of the two cars, there are also differences in where the weight is carried. The front/rear weight distribution of a coupe or convertible is 51/49, while the Z06 is 53/47. *Copyright 2003 GM Corp. Used with permission, GM Media Archive*

isn't spending his time working on powertrain engineering for new Corvettes, he moonlights as a well-respected restorer of old Corvettes. Nichols' knowledge of Corvette history allowed him to see the parallels between the hardcore enthusiast version of the C5 that he had helped develop and what Arkus-Duntov had in mind back in 1962.

The C5 Z06 can trace its immediate roots back to the 1999 introduction of the hardtop that completed the Corvette triumvirate. The hardtop was originally intended to provide a range of models that would accommodate the needs of everyone in the market. The targa-top hatchback targeted those wanting fun and functionality, and a no-frills hardtop would meet the needs of the entry-level high-performance sports car buyer.

Besides being the lightest C5 iteration by about 80 pounds, the hardtop also had the stiffest chassis, bettering the rigidity of the coupe by 12 percent. These are statistics that you would not expect to go unnoticed by the engineers in charge of designing America's premier performance car. By offering a base price that was $400 below that of the basic coupe model and a limited menu of extra-cost options, Hill's team had succeeded in meeting the original goal of a budget friendly Corvette. But why would they stop there? Why not reap the performance benefits of their C5 plan and give that stiffer chassis a workout by adding more power? After all, the new car market was booming, and buyers were looking for cars that delivered more, not less—especially in

terms of performance. The new direction for the hardtop was to develop it into a performance, not a price, leader. Therefore, why not let loose and build a real enthusiast's car?

"Even before we introduced the hardtop coupe in 1999, a couple of us [including Bill Nichols] who had some time, were working on a car—we didn't know what we would call it then," Tadge Juechter recalls. "We wanted to do something special and sell it to the [product] planners to make it official."

Starting with the light hardtop body, Hill's team trimmed even more weight by using a titanium exhaust system, lighter wheels and tires, and thinner window glass. When the Z06 first reappeared as a 2001 model, the only other production car with a titanium exhaust system was the million-dollar McLaren F1 super-exotic car. Even with air conditioning, stereo, and full power, the Z06 weighed 130 pounds less than a Corvette coupe or convertible.

What Chevrolet took out of the Z06, however, was not as interesting, or as much fun, as what they put in it. The Z06 had its own suspension setup featuring a larger front stabilizer bar, stiffer transverse-mounted rear leaf spring, and specific camber settings tuned for high-speed handling and control. The Z06 had wheels and tires unique from those of its siblings. Its distinctive

In 2003, the Bob Bondurant School of High Performance Driving acquired 16 C5 coupes and 4 Z06s to use as rolling classrooms. After having to practically rebuild the suspensions on the Mustangs to prepare them for his school, Bondurant was amazed at how little the C5 required to become "race ready." *Copyright 2003 GM Corp. Used with permission, GM Media Archive*

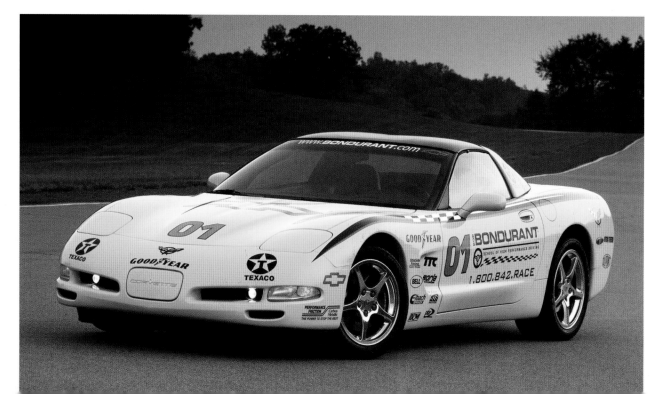

Thanks to lessons learned on tests at Germany's fabled Nurburgring, the 2004 Z06 zooms down the road with a suspension tweaked for better high-speed transitions on twisty roads. More apparent to non-drivers is the Le Mans Commemorative Edition paint scheme. *Copyright 2003 GM Corp. Used with permission, GM Media Archive*

cast alloy wheels were one inch wider front and rear to measure 17 x 9.5 inches up front and 18 x 10.5 inches at the rear. Riding on those rims were asymmetrical treaded tires (front: P265/40ZR17; rear: P295/35ZR18) that were custom designed by Goodyear for the Z06 application. The result of all this tinkering and tailoring was a nimble and responsive Corvette without the rock-hard ride of its predecessors.

The Z06 engine sported a name that was right out of the Chevy hall of fame. The first LS6 was a 1971 425-horsepower,

454-ci (7.4-liter) monster. It had a cast-iron block with aluminum heads. The latest LS6 not only featured aluminum heads, but also a cast-aluminum block and high-strength aluminum-alloy pistons. It showcased red engine covers for a pseudo-Testarossa look. The 5.7-liter LS6 debuted in the 2001 Z06 and produced 385 horsepower at 6,000 rpm. With a new camshaft, stronger valves, and improved engine breathing for 2002, output has moved beyond the magic 400 mark to hit 405 horsepower at 6,000 rpm.

Badges—we need those sparkling badges if we're going to have another special edition Corvette. This one celebrates the C5-R's attempt to get its third straight class win at Le Mans in 2003. You'll have to read the next chapter to discover what happened. *David Newhardt*

Proving that very little was left on the drafting table or in the parts drawers in developing the Z06, Corvette engineers left the Z06 alone for 2003. For 2004, they did a bit of fine-tuning and cosmetic work to reflect the model's racing heritage. Boosting its world-class performance image, the Z06 suspension was tightened to reduce the effects of roll and yaw during quick, transient maneuvers such as S-curves or a series of tight turns. The goal, as always, was to balance handling with ride comfort. This was primarily done by adjusting the shock-absorber valves to enhance both control and smoothness. Some of the test sessions that brought about these changes were carried out at what many consider to be the world's ultimate road racing course—the legendary Nordschleife (north trail) of Germany's

For once, what's under the hood is not as important as the hood itself. The RPO Z16 Z06 gets a carbon-fiber hood. At 20.5 pounds, it shaves off another 10.6 pounds of fat from the Z06. Unlike some manufacturers, Chevrolet worked hard to conceal the hood material, opting for a high-quality finish to the paint rather than following the boy-racer school of décor. Chevrolet did leave a tiny stripe of exposed carbon fiber next to the red piping. *David Newhardt*

The 2004 Commemorative Edition Z06 (RPO Z16) sports Le Mans Blue paint and silver stripes with red piping to emulate the paint job applied to the 2003 C5-R Le Mans cars. *David Newhardt*

Nürburgring. This high-speed circuit packs more than 170 curves in a lap that is just over 14 miles long. It also features elevation changes of nearly 1,000 feet achieved with steep uphill grades of 12 percent and roller-coaster-style drops of 11 percent. The Z06 is one of the few cars to have completed a lap of this torturous circuit in a time of under 8 minutes. The fastest lap ever turned at this track was a 6-minute, 11-second qualifying lap by Stefan Bellof in a Porsche 956 Le Mans-type racecar in 1983. Because of construction work that was being done that year, Bellof's lap time was set over a slightly modified course that was about 2 kilometers (1.2 miles) shorter than usual.

The 2004 Z06 was available in a Commemorative Edition (RPO Z16) that emulated the paint scheme of the 2004 C5-R that raced at Le Mans. It was painted Le Mans Blue with silver C5-R Le Mans striping, special badges, special seat embroidery, and polished, five-spoke aluminum wheels. Another racing-inspired addition was a carbon-fiber hood that weighed 20.5 pounds— 10.6 pounds less than the standard Z06 hood.

To achieve a glass-smooth finish for the hood, the carbon fiber was aligned in a single direction. Only the red border of the silver graphic on the hood bore the distinctive weave pattern that belies the exotic material used in manufacturing this hood.

Chevrolet sold only 199 copies of the original Z06. But with a price equivalent to a down payment on cars it can easily outrun, the new Z06 is as hard to pass in the showroom as it is on the road.

LS6: the heartbeat of the Z06

For 2001, the performance story for the standard Corvette LS1 V-8 was a 5 horsepower boost to 350 horsepower at 5,600 rpm along with more torque (360 ft-lb at 4,400 for automatics and 375 ft-lb at 4,400 for manual shifts). But grabbing the headlines of the C5 muscle news was the debut of the LS6 stuffed into the engine bay of the equally new Z06 model. Of course, you wouldn't have noticed much of a difference if you peeked under the respective hoods and compared a LS1-powered Corvette coupe or convertible to a Z06. Sure, there were the bright red engine covers atop the LS6, but unless you had X-ray vision, or a pocket dyno, things looked pretty similar.

The first iteration of the LS6 put out 385 horsepower at 6,000 rpm and an equivalent amount of torque at 4,800 rpm. That was almost a 12 percent jump over the LS1. The engine also carried a 6,500 rpm redline as opposed to the 6,000 rpm limit imposed on the LS1. So what magic did chief engineer Sam Winegarden,

assistant chief engineer John Juriga, and the rest of GM's small-block team perform under those red engine covers?

No sleight of hand was necessary—just good old-fashioned combustion engineering. Crankcase breathing was improved by deleting machined holes in the LS1 bulkhead and casting "windows" in the aluminum block to relieve backpressure that creates resistance as the pistons push air back toward the crankcase on their down stroke. These slots allowed the air to travel more freely between the crankcase bays, thus reducing resistance on piston travel, which can cause a loss in horsepower.

LS6 pistons are cast from high-strength, M142 aluminum alloy for enhanced durability. The pistons were also reshaped slightly from their LS1 counterparts, taking on a subtle barrel profile, to reduce friction. The aluminum cylinder heads of the LS6 were more precisely cast with special attention to the shape of the intake and exhaust ports. Smaller pent-roof combustion chambers

Be still my heart—the Z06 goes topless! Chuck Spielman of San Diego has, what was at the time of this photo session, the world's only Z06 convertible. Spielman is a Corvette collector and West Coast distributor for Advanced Automotive Technologies (AAT), a company known among C5 fanciers for the 1953/2003 Commemorative Edition Corvette. AAT converted his Z06 from a hardtop to a convertible. *David Newhardt*

AAT charges $15,000 to turn the hardtop into the convertible body. Since this is basically the reverse of what is done at Bowling Green, the change is not that complicated. Still, it is best handled by professionals like those at AAT in Michigan who use factory parts. The best part about this conversion is that you can really get an earful of that rumbling thunder from the titanium exhaust system. *David Newhardt*

that were smaller than the LS1 increased the compression ratio from 10.1:1 to 10.5:1. The net result was an increase in volumetric efficiency and more horsepower.

The biggest contributor to the horsepower gains of the LS6 was a steel-billet, high-lift camshaft that opened the valves quicker and longer to let more air flow into the combustion chamber. Higher-rate steel valve springs were used in conjunction with the cam to facilitate the opening and closing of the valves. Larger fuel injectors were also used to increase fuel flow in accordance with the increased airflow capacity of the engine. Fuel flow was increased by 10 percent over the LS1.

The LS6 also incorporated a unique crankcase ventilation system that consisted of an aluminum cover over the "V," or the valley between the heads. It featured composite oil baffles and integrated PCV plumbing. This high-performance ventilation system was designed to deal with the extreme cornering forces (over 1 lateral g) generated by the Z06 at the racetrack. The system not only reduced oil consumption, it also reduced the amount of external plumbing, thus reducing the potential for oil leaks. Still, some early 2001 LS6 engines did have problems with oil leakage

stemming from the seal of this cover. Chevrolet corrected this problem, and the affected engines were repaired under warranty.

The possibility that the LS6 could be operated at sustained high-speed levels raised questions about durability. As a concession, thin-wall, cast-iron exhaust manifolds replaced the previous stainless-steel manifolds. To further free up the heavy-breathing LS6, the engineers ventured into the loftier levels of exotic car technology by hanging on a titanium exhaust system that started just forward of the Z06 rear axle. Everything behind that point on the vehicle, including the low-restriction mufflers and the four 3.5-inch exhaust tips, was made of titanium. The system weighed half as much as the stainless-steel pieces used on the coupe and convertible. As a result, 17.6 pounds were lopped off the weight of a Z06. This was the first-ever use of titanium in the exhaust system of a regular production car (the limited-production McLaren F1 exotic sports car also used titanium).

Dave Hill says the original goal for the LS6 was to get to the magic 400 horsepower number. So no one (with the exception of some of the 5,773 people who bought a 2001 Z06) was disappointed when the small-block engineering team exceeded that goal by coming up with another 20 horses for the 2002 LS6. The power then topped out at 405 horsepower at 6,000 rpm with torque improving to 400 ft-lb at 4,800 rpm. Sam Winegarden referred to the work of John Juriga and his staff as "the ruthless pursuit of horsepower."

Some suspect that the 20 horsepower jump between the 2001 and 2002 Z06 was more of a marketing ploy than an engineering change. But Winegarden admits that the real reason for the change was that certain valvetrain issues in the development of such a high-revving OHV engine were not adequately resolved before the 2001 production date. The decision was therefore made to follow a two-step process in the development of the LS6.

The changes for 2002 revolved around making the LS6 even freer breathing by utilizing a revised air cleaner housing, a low restriction mass airflow (MAF) sensor, lightweight valves, a higher-lift camshaft, and a modified exhaust. The revised LS6 gulped down more outside air through a larger opening (by about 6.65 square inches) in the new air box. This increased volume of air enjoyed a less impeded path to the intake manifold thanks to the less restrictive MAF sensor.

Beginning in 2002, new lighter-weight, hollow-stem valves contributed to lowering valvetrain mass to reduce valve "flutter" at high rpm. Exhaust valves were filled with a liquid-sodium alloy for better heat transference that led to better engine cooling.

The star of the 2002 LS6 power show was the new cam that increased valve lift by 0.7 millimeters, allowing more intake and exhaust flow through the combustion chamber. The induction-hardened cam was stronger and better balanced than its predecessor. Use of an advanced opto-electrical process for inspecting the camshaft assured extremely high quality.

Last, but not least, exhaust flow was increased by eliminating the dual catalytic converters without affecting the ability to meet NLEV emission standards.

The custom interior of Chuck Spielman's Z06 convertible cost about $4,000 more. The price includes richer feeling leather seats and trim. Work was done by Vette Essentials, which is near the AAT shops in Rochester Hills, Michigan. *David Newhardt*

SPECIAL EFFECTS:
what sets the Z06 apart from its C5 siblings

The LS6 and the hardtop body configuration were the two major things that set the Z06 apart from the less intense offerings in the C5 catalog. The Z06 also had its own version of the six-speed manual transmission (the M12 as opposed to the M6) which had more aggressive gearing and was built to handle the added strain from the LS6. The rear portion of the Z06 exhaust system was titanium, not stainless steel, and had four 3.5-inch exhaust tips.

The FE4 suspension was unique to the Z06. It included a larger, hollow, 30-millimeter front stabilizer bar, a stiffer rear leaf spring (125N/millimeter versus 113N/millimeter of the Z51), and greater negative camber settings front and rear. The Z06 had aluminum wheels (front, 17 x 9.5 inches; rear, 18 x 10.5 inches) that were 1 inch wider, at the front and the rear than a standard C5. Special Goodyear Eagle F1 SC tires (front, P265/40ZR-17; rear, P295/35ZR-18) were developed specifically for the Z06. Besides being larger and having a higher-performance-oriented tread pattern, the tires also shaved 23.4 pounds off the unsprung weight of the Z06 to further sharpen handling and response. These tires were not of run-flat construction, so the standard Corvette tire-pressure monitoring system was not used. Since there was no spare tire, a special tire-inflator kit was supplied. It consisted of a miniature air compressor and a squeeze bottle of latex-based tire sealer.

External changes to the Z06 included functional air inlets in the front fascia to supply cool air to the intake system. Air scoops on the rear rocker panels provided cooling air to the rear brakes. These were said to reduce rear brake temperatures by as much as 10 percent. Speaking of the brakes, the front calipers were painted red.

The Z06 boasted its own instrument cluster with special checkerboard graphics and a tachometer with a 6,500-rpm redline. The seats featured additional side bolstering to better secure both driver and passenger when the enhanced cornering capabilities were put to the test. The Z06 logo was embroidered on the headrests.

Z06 VERSUS C5 MANUAL GEARBOX

GEAR RATIOS	LS1/MM6	LS6/M12
1st	2.66:1 (51mph)	2.97:1 (48mph)
2nd	1.78:1 (76)	2.07:1 (69)
3rd	1.30:1 (104)	1.43:1 (100)
4th	1.00:1 (136)	1.00:1 (143)
5th	0.74:1 (175)	0.84:1 (171)
6th	0.50:1 N/A	0.56:1 N/A
Reverse	2.90:1	3.28:1

(Speed at Redline)

2001 Z06 PERFORMANCE VERSUS 2001 C5 COUPE/CONVERTIBLE

TRANSMISSION	AXLE RATIO	0-60 MPH	1/4 ELAPSED TIME
Z06 M12	3.42:1	4.00 seconds	12.60 seconds
M30 4-speed automatic	2.73:1	4.90 seconds	13.65 seconds
M30 4-speed automatic	3.15:1	4.75 seconds	13.50 seconds
MM6 6-speed manual	3.42:1	4.55 seconds	13.25 seconds

speed is relative in the corvette family

The slogan on a popular T-shirt worn by maturing racers quips, "The older I get, the faster I was." The same thinking applies to the potent Corvettes of the past. The 1971 454-ci, 425-horsepower, LS6-equipped Corvette did zero to 60 miles per hour in 5.3 seconds and had a quarter-mile time of 13.8 seconds at 105 miles per hour. The other muscular Corvette of that era, a 1967 427-ci, 435-horsepower Stingray was clocked at 5.5 seconds from zero to 60 and matched the LS6 time down the drag strip. Chevy's numbers for the 375-horsepower, 1990 ZR-1 "King of the Hill" version of the Corvette erased almost a second off those zero to 60 times, coming in at 4.9 seconds. The ZR1 hustled through the quarter-mile in 13.4 seconds. Chevy quoted zero to 60 speeds for the new Z06 as 4.0 seconds flat with a quarter-mile elapsed time of 12.6 seconds at 114 miles per hour.

driving impressions of the 2002 z06

Forget all that stuff about those who fail to learn from history being doomed to repeat it. Repeating history is a foot-stomping, arm-twisting, neck-snapping delight when you're in the cockpit of a 2002 Corvette Z06.

Nestle into the firmly bolstered, high-back leather seats, and you'll find it's easy to envision yourself in one of the racing C5-R Corvettes that won its class at Le Mans in 2001. The six-speed manual shifter is close at hand, sprouting up from the elbow-high center console. The transmission feels stiff and becomes recalcitrant at times about going into reverse, but that only adds to the race car atmosphere. Sparse insulation lets you fully enjoy the sound of America's racing national anthem as played by the quick-to-rev Chevy V-8. It is a glorious tune that will have you stabbing the throttle just to revel in it.

There are 405 horses corralled under the red valve covers of the freer breathing version of the LS6 introduced in 2002. They provide sufficient motivation for the Z06 to flirt with zero to 60-mile-per-hour times under 4 seconds. The car offers the kind of performance you'd typically expect from a Porsche Turbo, and it's available for less than half the price. And Chevy throws in a thunderous V-8 bellow that the Porsche can't match at any price. Chevy claims top speed is a bit over 171 miles per hour.

While the acceleration may be brutish, the Z06 handling comes off as refined. The only blemish is that the speed-sensitive

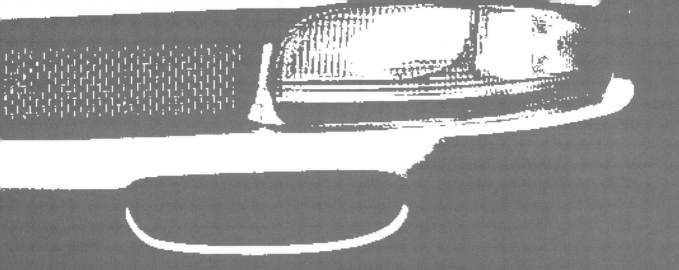

rack-and-pinion steering could provide more road feel. The Active Handling system features a console-mounted "on/off" switch, otherwise known as the "fun" button. It permits you to disengage the traction control for track use. Turning off the traction control allows you to use the throttle, and the 405 horses it manages, as a steering device to hustle the Z06 on tight, wriggly courses. With the traction control off, you can perform a high-speed balancing act typically enjoyed by the owners of older Porsche 911s. Those Corvette forays to Le Mans certainly have had a positive effect on the handling properties of America's sports car icon.

The Z06 also impresses with its absence of the usual creaks, rattles, and groans one expects to encounter while driving one of Chevy's fiberglass creations. Panel fit and finish is also much improved over past Corvettes. In addition to its construction virtues, the Z06's leaner, meaner hardtop styling, accentuated by brake cooling ducts ahead of the rear wheels, de-emphasizes the C5 Corvette's hefty derriere. The Z06 is only available in the hardtop configuration, which features a more vertical, fixed rear window. Conversely, for 2002, the only hardtops are Z06s.

The Z06 is not as visually dynamic inside as it is outside. The good news is that Chevrolet has finally given up on the arcade game that passed as an instrument panel in the C4. It's back to the basics after the experiment with the half-digital, half-analog arrangement. Centered in front of the Z06 driver is a large round speedometer and a similar sized tachometer with a 6,500-rpm redline that tell you all you really need to know. A quartet of smaller auxiliary gauges flanks either side of the two main dials. And, surprisingly, located on the passenger side of the dash is a real, useable glove box. The new instrument panel isn't the most attractive, and it is heavy on the plastic, but at least everything does its job with a minimum of fuss and confusion.

Chevrolet could not resist adding one glitzy gizmo to remind everyone that the Corvette is its technical tour de force. That special addition is the Head-Up Display (HUD). It's a jet fighter-style information display screen that appears as an eerie, green specter floating on the lower windshield directly in front of the driver. It is standard on the Z06 and features digital speed read-out, oil pressure, and a tiny tachometer that wraps around two borders of the roughly 2-inch-square screen. You have the option of turning HUD off, but it'll seem less intrusive over time. Plus, being able to watch your speed and the road at the same time can come in handy when cruising past school zones or donut shops—not that you'd want to spend all that much time meandering around the neighborhood in a Z06. It's one car that's ready to race to and from as well as at the track.

2002 Z06 Specifications

Engine	5.7-liter OHV aluminum V-8
Power	405 horsepower at 6,000 rpm
Torque	400 ft-lb at 4,800 rpm
0-to-60 Time	4.0 seconds
Top Speed	171 miles per hour
Transmission	Six-speed manual
Wheelbase	104.5 inches
Curb Weight	3,118 pounds
Fuel Economy	19 miles per gallon city/28 miles per gallon highway
Base Price	$49,705
Options	Millennium Yellow $600; Corvette Museum Delivery, Bowling Green, KY $490

school tool
bob bondurant is a combination
"old school" and "new school" z06 racer.

Bob Bondurant is certainly well schooled when it comes to racing Corvettes. The man who popularized and perfected the art of high-performance driving instruction—teaching over 90,000 students since 1968—was a championship Corvette racer in the late 1950s and early 1960s. In 1962, Bondurant was one of the drivers tapped by Chevrolet to drive one of the first factory-prepped Z06 racers.

Bondurant had raced in Corvettes sponsored by Washburn Chevrolet, a dealership in Santa Barbara, California. Washburn wanted to buy a Z06, but Chevrolet would not sell him one unless Bondurant would drive it.

"They are building four of them, but they are not, " Bondurant remembers Washburn telling him over the phone, alluding to the top-secret, back-door nature of Chevy's racing program at the time. "They won't sell me one unless you drive it."

Bondurant picked up the Z06 at the factory and drove it cross country to California where it debuted at Riverside.

"I had a great time," he says of the trip. "I had a buddy with me so we drove straight through. I don't remember how long it took, but we were flying!"

Bondurant dropped off his friend and was nearly home when he decided to give the Z06 one last, quick blast through the gears.

"I was thinking, 'This is great,'" says Bondurant. "So I stepped on the gas along Sunset Boulevard, and here comes a motorcycle cop going the other way. I saw he was on the binders real hard so I slowed down, but he still gave me a ticket. Son of a gun, I almost made it all the way home."

Bondurant recalls the Z06 as looking "just like a stock car, but it was pretty much a race car underneath."

He also says that it was definitely a better car than the previous solid-axle Corvettes he raced—and it was quicker.

"It was a good car, a really good car," he says. "We were the only Corvette that could stay with the Cobras, but we could never beat 'em because they were a bit lighter, and they had better brakes. We could out-corner them, but we couldn't out-brake them to make a pass."

Bondurant finally out-qualified the Cobras at a race in Pomona. His pole position went for naught when his fuel injection started leaking on the trip to the grid.

"We never had a problem with the car, but the smog had eaten the rubber in the O-rings, and fuel was everywhere."

After a call for help over the public address system, two spectators volunteered the use of the fuel-injection parts from their street Corvettes. But the time wasted doing the repairs left Bondurant behind the pack at the start.

"I finally caught up near the end but still couldn't pass the Cobras. I think Shelby was afraid that the Corvette was getting close to beating the Cobra. He called me and had me driving Ken Miles' Cobra two weeks later."

Bondurant went on to great success driving Cobras for Shelby in Europe, but he still has happy memories of driving the original Z06.

Now, 40 years later, he has been reunited with the newest Z06 at his Bob Bondurant School of High Performance Driving near Phoenix. Ironically, this time around he is switching from Ford to Chevy. Sixteen C5s and four Z06s are replacing specially built Ford Mustangs as the school's rolling classrooms.

"Roush Racing had to build those Mustangs for us to make it handle," says Bondurant. "The Corvette is a much better car to start with. All I've done is put on a little bigger rear sway bar. Even without it, the car handles real good, but the rear sway bar dials it in perfect."

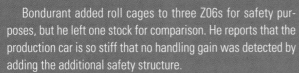

Bondurant added roll cages to three Z06s for safety purposes, but he left one stock for comparison. He reports that the production car is so stiff that no handling gain was detected by adding the additional safety structure.

As for the C5 versus Z06 comparison, Bondurant says, "The Z06 is lighter and has 50 more horsepower so it's quicker. The handling is very similar, but mainly it's quicker."

Bondurant starts all students out with the traction control engaged.

"I can take the Z06 with the traction control on and turn some really hot laps and never get into it [the traction control]. The way you drive a Corvette, especially the Z06, you drive it with a smooth throttle on and off. If you jump on it, then you need the traction control. It's got so much torque, if you just squeeze the gas nice and smooth, it works fantastic, and it's quick."

Because of the extremes he puts his cars through in the brutal desert heat, Bondurant has added additional cooling for the engine and transmission—and with no problems.

When it comes to the performance and durability of his Corvette fleet, Bondurant proclaims that he's a "happy camper"—and his campground is the 1.6-mile, 15-turn road course he's designed for his driving school. So far, the C5 is getting straight "A"s from the head professor.

Bob Bondurant puts one of his new Z06 "school cars" through the paces on the track he personally designed for his racing school near Phoenix. Other than extra coolers to handle the extreme desert heat, a rollcage, and a new rear stabilizer bar, the Z06 was ready to work right out of the box. *Rick Scuteri*

chapter five
R is for RACE...
and RESULTS

the beginnings

The fifth-generation Corvette was not only the best to hit the highways, its racing version was by far the best Corvette to ever hit the racetrack. The C5's racing career got off to a flying start in Long Beach, California, in April 1998. Paul Gentilozzi drove the first competition-prepared C5 through the downtown street course for a flag-to-flag win in the Trans-Am series season opener. Gentilozzi's wide, black C5 would win six more races that year to give him his first Trans-Am driver's championship—the first one for a Corvette driver since 1981. Chevrolet also won the Trans-Am manufacturer's championship.

Although Corvettes had raced at Le Mans in the past (Briggs Cunningham being the first Corvette entrant in 1960), the two C5-Rs that went over in 2000 were the first factory-backed effort in history. Ron Fellows, Chris Kneifel, and Justin Bell in #63 finished 11th overall. Their sister car finished 10th.

It wasn't a bad introduction to racing, but remember that the C5 was launched with much loftier, world-class goals. Its aspirations were to compete with sports cars like Porsches and Ferraris. And to do that, it needed to race where Porsches and Ferraris race—international endurance races such as the Daytona 24 Hours, Sebring, and the *grand-père* of them all, the 24 Hours of Le Mans.

Corvettes had raced at Le Mans before, beginning in 1960 when Briggs Cunningham entered a quartet of them. One of them finished eighth overall. Many other Corvette entrants followed Cunningham's lead down through the years, but no one was able to match that top 10 finish—at least not until the C5-R arrived.

The factory-backed C5-R program began just about the time that the C5 road car was getting ready to make its debut. Corvette racing program manager Doug Fehan contacted Gary Pratt of Pratt & Miller Engineering and Fabrication in Wixom, Michigan, and told him of Chevrolet's desire to race the C5. Pratt had a long history of building successful road racers including Corvettes for John Greenwood, Trans-Am Camaros for Ron Fellows, and a number of IMSA cars including GTO- and GTP-class Mustangs as well as the Intrepid GTP racer. Pratt began investigating the C5's potential with an eye toward competing at Le Mans.

1999

Before packing up and heading overseas, however, Chevrolet committed to a long-term plan that would develop the C5-R in long-distance races in America before heading across the pond to do battle. The C5-R made its racing debut in January 1999 at the Daytona 24 Hours race. John Paul Jr., Chris Kneifel, and Ron Fellows drove one of two C5-Rs entered in the GT2 class and ran as high as fifth overall for a quarter of the race. Then an oil fitting broke, causing the Corvette to become a rolling version of the Exxon Valdez. Officials black-flagged the car into the pits for repairs. After a lengthy stop and some hard work by the crew, plus many big bags of "kitty litter" to sop up the oil slick, the Goodwrench-sponsored car returned to finish third in its class and 18th overall. A sister car finished 12th in class, although in 46th position overall.

The C5-Rs were fast, but their GT-class competition, primarily Porsches and Vipers, had better reliability and outlasted them to win races. The best finish for a Corvette in the five races entered during 1999 was a second in class at Laguna Seca. By the way, a C5 did go over to Le Mans in 1999. Corvette was the official pace car for the 67th running of the French endurance racing classic.

2000

In 2000, Corvette prepared to race for real at Le Mans as well as at seven events in the United States, starting again with the Daytona 24 Hours in January. Gone was the black-and-silver Goodwrench paint scheme. The new yellow paint brought with it a sunny future for the C5-R. At the road course that includes some of the high banks of the legendary Daytona Speedway, the C5-R qualified first in its class, ahead of the factory Vipers. In 35 years of racing at Daytona, the highest finish for a Corvette had been third overall in 1973. With one hour left in the 2000 race, the last of the faster prototype cars had dropped out, and the race for the overall victory became a battle between the leading GT-class cars, a Viper, and Ron Fellows in the C5-R. When the checkered flag fell, the C5-R crossed the finish stripe a mere 31 seconds behind the winning Viper after 24 hours of hard-fought racing. It wasn't quite a victory, but the C5-R did become the highest-finishing Corvette in Daytona history.

By the time two cars were entered at Sebring in March, almost 5,000 miles of testing had been accumulated. Despite the preparation and the high hopes carried over from Daytona, the best they could do was a fifth in class. The next stop was Le Mans in June.

The first-ever factory-backed Corvette team at Le Mans was ready to take on the Vipers that had been racing there for five years and had won the GTS class in 1998 and 1999. In qualifying, a Viper grabbed the pole, but the two C5-Rs took second and

A fleet of Millennium Yellow C5 convertibles accompanied the C5-Rs to Le Mans for use by GM VIPs during the weekend. The cars were then ferried across France back to Paris by a group of journalists, including the author, who stopped along the way to visit the old racing circuit near Reims. The French loved the sight of the big yellow American sports cars on the track and on the road. Leaving Le Mans after the race, the *gendarmes* were more intent on snapping pictures of the Corvettes than directing traffic.

Corvette racing is not a 9-to-5 job. Pratt & Miller Engineering and Fabrication not only builds the C5-Rs, it also provides race support. Here the crew services the car during a stop at the 12 Hours of Sebring. *Copyright 2003 GM Corp. Used with permission, GM Media Archive*

third ahead of the two other Vipers. Ron Fellows, Chris Kneifel, and Justin Bell were in the first car (#63) while Andy Pilgrim, Kelly Collins, and Franck Freon drove the second (#64).

Despite the sizzling weather conditions, the two Corvettes were fighting for second in class at the 20-hour mark. In the last hour, the #64 car encountered a bit of drama during its pit stop when the starter gave out. After a quick repair, the car resumed the race to finish 10th overall and third in class. The #63 car finished right behind it in 11th overall and fourth in class. It wasn't a bad first effort. The French, and anyone else who heard the booming American V-8s blast down the long Mulsanne Straight, fell in love with the big and raucous American sports cars.

Things continued to improve once the cars got back home. After coming in second to the Viper by a mere 0.354 of a second in August at Mosport, the C5-R seemed poised to take its first victory. That came a month later at Texas Motor Speedway

when it was the Vipers' turn to suffer mechanical problems, and Ron Fellows charged to a three-lap victory margin.

"The snake has been bitten," screamed Fellows from the top step of the podium.

Hoping to prove its win at Texas was not a fluke, the C5-R team entered two cars at the 10-hour-long Petite Le Mans at Road Atlanta in October. Both cars broke the existing GTS-class lap record in qualifying to start one-two. With an hour left in the race, the class leader was Tommy Archer in a Viper about 14 seconds ahead of Andy Pilgrim in the #4 Corvette. Fellows' #3 had dropped a cylinder but was still limping along in third. With two laps to go, Pilgrim had moved up to Archer's rear bumper and, when Archer moved outside to defend his lead in turn one, Pilgrim slipped under him for the pass and went on to victory. The C5-R's sophomore racing season ended with two wins, three seconds, and a great showing at Le Mans.

2001

It turned out that once the C5-R got a taste of victory, there was no holding it back. The year 2001 would be a very memorable and historic one for Corvette racing fans.

At the Daytona 24 Hours, the Corvette team included two "guest" drivers. Dale Earnhardt and his son, Dale Earnhardt Jr., were paired up with Kelly Collins and Andy Pilgrim in the yellow #3 (what else?) C5-R. A second car, #2, was driven by Fellows, Freon, Kneifel, and Johnny O'Connell. Both Big E and Little E were Corvette owners—Dale driving a black 1998 C5, while Jr. opted for a 1999 red C5 coupe. Little E also owns a red 1971 454 convertible. At the time, both men had ordered specially modified Z06s that had 480-horsepower engines and bodywork resembling the C5-R.

The 2001 edition of the Daytona 24 Hours was one of the wettest in history. The Earnhardts impressed with both their driving skill on the road course and their team spirit. The senior Earnhardt not only felt at ease doing 175 miles per hour in the rain, he begged for more seat time.

The #2 car driven by Fellows assumed the overall lead with 3-1/2 hours to go and cruised to an 8-lap victory, becoming the first Corvette to be the overall winner. The #3 car wound up in fourth place overall but second in its class. Sadly, just 14 days later Dale Earnhardt would be killed in a last lap accident at the Daytona 500 on this same track.

The Daytona race was not the end of the team's success in 24-hour races that year. The 20 hours of rain that the team

The year 2001 got off to a great start for the C5-R at the Daytona 24 Hours. Guest drivers Dale Earnhardt and his son shared a car with Andy Pilgrim and Kelly Collins. The #2 car of Ron Fellows became the first Corvette to capture an overall victory at the historic race. The car driven by the Earnhardts finished fourth overall, but second in class to the #2 car. As a result, both teams shared the GTS-class podium. Sadly, Dale Earnhardt would be killed racing his stock car at this track 14 days later. *Copyright 2003 GM Corp. Used with permission, GM Media Archive*

Kelly Collins, Andy Pilgrim, and Franck Freon drove the C5-R #64 to the runner-up position behind their teammates. They would finish 14th overall. Note the black Grand Sport-style racing stripe on the fender in memory of Dale Earnhardt.

sloshed through to win Daytona was the best preparation of all for their return to Le Mans. A sudden downpour just after the traditional 4:00 P.M. start not only created havoc in the running order, but also proved to be a harbinger of the weather conditions to follow during the night and through most of the next day. Fellows, O'Connell, and Scott Pruett were in the yellow #63, while Collins, Freon, and Pilgrim teamed to drive the #64. When the 24-hour period was up, the mud-caked cars looked more brown than yellow, but they had soldiered on to a one-two finish in their class. The #63 finished 8th overall to equal the best finish ever for a Corvette at Le Mans, while the #64 car came in a credible 14th.

The C5-R would also pick up GTS-class wins in six of eight American Le Mans Series races run in 2001 to earn that series' GTS-class manufacturers' championship.

The C5-R #63 lined up on the pre-grid before the 4:00 P.M. Saturday start of the 24-hour race. Drivers Ron Fellows, Johnny O'Connell, and Scott Pruett would eventually slog through 20 hours of rainy weather before winning the GTS class and coming in 8th overall. That finish would equal the best finish ever for a Corvette at Le Mans.

The car may be covered in mud, but it's still running strong. The Corvette #63 goes through the Porsche Curves after surviving the night and the wet weather.

2002

It was déjà vu all over again, only better, during the 2002 racing season. Unfortunately, a new sanctioning body had diluted both the quality and prestige of the Daytona 24 Hours. The Corvette team would skip the race in order to better prepare for an expanded schedule of American Le Mans Series (ALMS) events plus Le Mans itself. The season opener was at another historic Florida endurance race, the 12 Hours of Sebring. Ron Fellows, Johnny O'Connell, and Oliver Gavin were impressive in driving their #3 Corvette to an eight-lap GTS-class win over a strong field of Vipers, Saleens, and a 550 Ferrari Maranello.

Pictured is the Pratt & Miller Corvette racing team at Le Mans in 2002. Gary Pratt leans against #64, while Jim Miller sits on #63. *Copyright 2003 GM Corp. Used with permission, GM Media Archive*

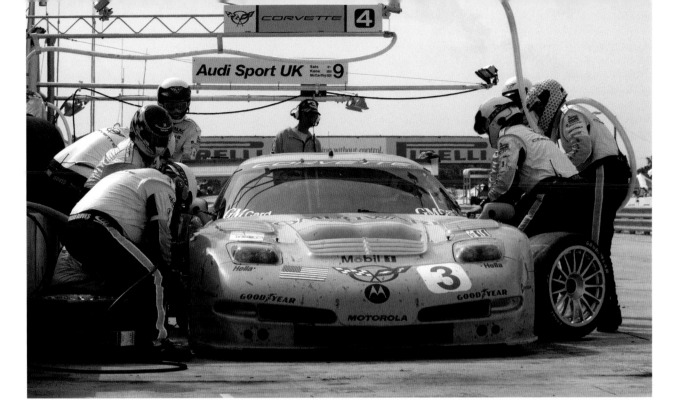

The 2002 season opener was at the 12 Hours of Sebring endurance race where #3, driven by Fellows, O'Connell, and Gavin, scored an impressive eight-lap victory in the GTS class. *Copyright 2003 GM Corp. Used with permission, GM Media*

In 2002, the Prodrive Ferrari Maranello started to creep up on the CR-5 in the GTS class at Le Mans and in the American Le Mans Series (ALMS). By Le Mans 2003, it would be the Corvettes chasing after the Ferrari. *Copyright 2003 GM Corp. Used with permission, GM Media Archive*

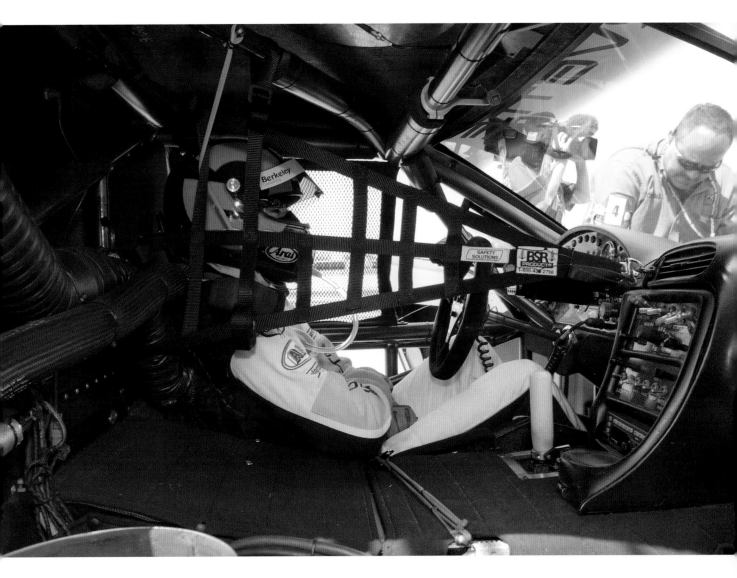

And you thought the C4 had a cramped interior. The Pi Research information display replaces the stock instrumentation. Various switches and a two-way radio take the place of the stereo and climate control systems in the center stack. *Copyright 2003 GM Corp. Used with permission, GM Media Archive*

The Ferrari would prove to be tough competition for the Corvettes at Le Mans. By the 12th hour of racing on the over eight-mile-long circuit that includes portions of rural French highways, the Ferrari had built up a two-lap lead over the two C5-Rs. An oil fire sidelined the Ferrari, and the Corvettes soldiered on for their second consecutive 1-2 class win at Le Mans.

Corvettes would also be repeat winners of the ALMS GTS-class manufacturers' championship by winning nine of ten ALMS races. In addition, Ron Fellows would be first in the ALMS GTS-class driver's championship.

2003

Fellows, O'Connell, and Freon kicked off the 2003 season by winning the GTS class at the 12 Hours of Sebring using a 2002-spec C5-R chassis. A new 2003 chassis, and a new red-white-and-blue paint job, made its debut at Le Mans.

Like its predecessors, the latest race chassis still used production C5 hydroformed frame rails, but it was stiffer and a little lighter than the previous C5-R. Extensive wind tunnel tests had come up with aerodynamic improvements to the front fascia, the undertray, and rear diffuser to increase downforce and reduce drag. On the engine front, improvements to the induction system were made to increase throttle response and low-end torque. Air restrictors imposed by the rules limited the engine to about 620 horsepower.

In honor of the Corvette's 50th anniversary, the two C5-Rs wore #50 and #53 at Le Mans. Unfortunately, the change in numbers and the new paint jobs would not help the C5-R get the hat trick at Le Mans. Just as the Corvette had done in 2000,

the Ferrari Maranello had returned to Le Mans in 2003 with reliability to match its impressive speed, and it took the GTS-class win. Despite a number of problems, including a stop by the #50 on the very first lap to repair the throttle linkage, the two C5-Rs and their determined crews never gave up, and the cars hung on to finish second and third in their class behind the Ferrari.

The C5-R racing story does not end here. While a third straight class win at Le Mans did not happen, the Corvettes returned to the United States with high hopes for winning a third straight ALMS GTS class championship.

For Le Mans 2003, the C5-Rs had a new sponsor, Compuware, and a new paint job. The Le Mans Blue paint also appears on Le Mans Commemorative Edition production C5s. New numbers are also applied for 2003 effort — #50 and #53 celebrate the Corvette's 50th anniversary. *Copyright 2003 GM Corp. Used with permission, GM Media Archive*

The 2003 C5-Rs headed back to Le Mans with all the new paint, logos, and numbers and sporting a more aerodynamic nose and front splitter. Their attempt to notch a third straight class victory came up short. Alternator problems on #53 and a stop to repair the throttle linkage at the start by car #50 slowed the Corvette effort. The Prodrive Ferrari Maranello came in first by being both faster and more reliable. *Copyright 2003 GM Corp. Used with permission, GM Media Archive*

building the PERFECT beast:
a LOOK inside the C5-R

So how different is the C5-R from that Millennium Yellow Z06 in your driveway? Well, they both start out with hydroformed side rails. The C5-R uses these as the foundation for the roll cage. The new power steering pump and steering rack are the same as stock, as are the windshield, taillights, and marker lights. The stock suspension cradles are also used but altered to accept the race-modified suspension pieces. The suspension arms are longer, and the transverse springs have been eliminated in favor of adjustable coil-over shocks. The anti-roll bars are also adjustable.

The engine displacement went up to about 7.0 liters thanks to an increase in the bore and stroke. The engineers at Katech, Inc., who build the motors that go into the Pratt & Miller-built chassis, installed a forged billet crankshaft, forged connecting rods and pistons, a racing cam, and a high-performance valve-train. A special racing fuel-injection system is also used. New for 2003 was a sequential shift transmission.

The sophisticated driver information system of the Z06 was replaced by an even more sophisticated Pi Research dashboard display that monitors assorted temperatures and pressures as well as computing lap times and fuel use.

If all this sounds like something you can use, Pratt & Miller will sell you a customer version of the C5-R that will set you back around $440,000. It's guaranteed to get you to work a lot faster.

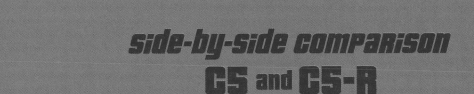

side-by-side comparison
C5 and C5-R

DIMENSIONS	2000 CORVETTE C5	CORVETTE C5-R
Wheelbase	104.5 inches	104.7 inches
Length	179.7 inches	182.8 inches
Width	73.6 inches	76.4 inches
Height	47.7 inches	45.8 inches
Front Tread	62.1 inches	74.7 inches
Rear Tread	62.2 inches	76.1 inches

DIMENSIONS	2000 CORVETTE C5	CORVETTE C5-R
Curb Weight	3,245 pounds (coupe)	2,510 pounds
Fuel Capacity	18.5 U.S. gallons (70 liters)	26.4 U.S. gallons (70 liters)
Structure/Frame	Steel-welded perimeter frame with hydroformed rails	Steel-welded perimeter frame with hydroformed rails
Body	Fiberglass-reinforced plastic	Carbon fiber
Front and Rear Suspension	Upper and lower A-arms, transverse leaf spring, gas shocks, anti-roll bar	Upper and lower A-arms, coil-over adjustable springs, adjustable shocks, adjustable anti-roll bar
Front Tires/Wheels	P245/45ZR17 Goodyear Eagle F-1 EMT/17x8.5-inch aluminum	25x12-18 Goodyear Racing Eagle/BBS forged magnesium center lock 18x12.5-inch
Rear Tires/Wheels	P275/40ZR18 Goodyear Eagle F-1 EMT/18x9.5-inch aluminum	28x14-18 Goodyear Racing Eagle/BBS forged magnesium center lock 18x13-inch
Brake Type	4-wheel vented disc w/ABS	4-wheel vented carbon disc; AP monoblock calipers
Front Rotor Diameter/Thickness	12.6 inches/1.26 inches	15.0 inches/1.38 inches
Rear Rotor Diameter/Thickness	11.8 inches/1.0 inches	14.0 inches/1.26 inches
Total Swept Area Front/Rear	263 sq. in./158 sq. in.	343 sq. in./292 sq. in
Engine	LS1 ohv 2-valve/cyl. V-8	LS1 ohv 2-valve/cyl. V-8
Displacement	5.67 liters (346-ci)	6.98 liters (427-ci)
Bore X Stroke	3.90 x 3.62 inches	4.124 x 4.00 inches
Compression Ratio	10.1:1	12.5:1
Horsepower	345 at 5,600 rpm	620 at 6,400 rpm
Torque	350 ft-lb at 4,400 rpm	495 ft-lb at 5,200 rpm
Transmission	Six-speed manual or four-speed automatic	Six-speed or five-speed manual

RVGTTG

chapter six
C5 SPECIALS:
if you have the scratch, these guys can take care of the itch

guldstrand signature edition anniversary corvette

The Corvette's 50th anniversary spurred a number of special editions. Dick Guldstrand has been associated with fast Corvettes for almost as many years as there have been Corvettes, so it was not surprising that this member of the Corvette Hall of Fame created one of the most powerful anniversary specials.

Guldstrand salutes the Corvette's past and present by taking a Z06 and stuffing it with a 427-ci motor. In keeping with the anniversary theme, Guldstrand said he would only build 50 of his Signature Edition cars and sell them through authorized Chevy dealers for $49,330, plus a 2003 Z06.

The New Generation 427 engine supplied by Guldstrand was built by Katech, Inc., the same company that supplies the Le Mans class-winning powerplants of the C5-R. Katech started out with the stock 5.7-liter V-8 of the Z06 and increased the bore to 4.1 inches by installing its own cylinder sleeves and pistons.

Katech lengthened the stroke to 4.0 inches by installing Carillo rods and a 4340 forged crankshaft. The block was re-machined for the added strength, which was supplied by billet steel main caps plus head and main bearing studs of the same material.

Combustion chambers were cc'd and ported and topped by Katech Stage III cylinder heads. The compression ratio was raised to 10.8:1. Rocker arms and lifters remained stock, but did their work with titanium retainers and stainless steel valves plus an adjustable high-performance timing chain from the C5-R. The camshaft profile was altered for increased lift and longer duration without negatively impacting drivability. A Katech ported throttle body supplied the fuel. At the opposite end of the combustion cycle, a Flowmaster exhaust system helped the engine exhale spent gasses.

What all these modifications added up to was 500 horsepower at 5,600 rpm and 520 ft-lb of torque at 4,700 rpm.

To keep all this power going in the intended direction, Guldstrand installed 1.5-inch front and 1.0-inch rear stabilizer bars with Heim-jointed links along with Michelin Pilot Sport tires (front:

The stickers on the carbon fiber valve covers tell you almost everything you need to know about why this C5 is a special edition. Corvette racer, tuner, and hall of famer Dick Guldstrand has stuffed a 427-ci engine inside a C5 to celebrate Corvette's 50th anniversary. Katech, Inc., the company that supplies the motors for the C5-R, is building the engines for the Guldstrand anniversary specials. The bored-and-stroked LS1 puts out an even 500 horsepower. *Dick Guldstrand*

Special rear-end treatment includes a trailing edge lip spoiler, European-style taillight lenses, and revised rear fascia. Fikse Profil 10 wheels are 18 x 10 inches in front and 19 x 11 inches at the rear. Guldstrand claims the car has been clocked at 12.4 seconds in the quarter-mile. *Dick Guldstrand*

The interior package includes a carbon fiber center console; blue suede accents on the steering wheel, shifter, and door panels; plus re-contoured sport seats trimmed in gold leather and blue suede with embroidered Guldstrand logos. *Dick Guldstrand*

275/35ZR18; rear: 295/35ZR19) on Fikse Profil 10 wheels, sized at widths of 10 and 11 inches respectively.

Guldstrand stuck with the factory-associated theme on the outside, employing styling touches such as a power dome hood, a revised rear fascia with Euro-style taillights, and graphics dreamed up by former GM designer John Schinella. The paint scheme used DuPont Anniversary Gold and Cobalt Blue.

The interior reflected this color scheme in suede and leather on the re-contoured seats with embossed logos. Other added touches included a carbon fiber center console and blue suede accents on the door panels, shift lever, and steering wheel.

Callaway C12

When the Callaway C12 first appeared at the Geneva International Automobile Salon in March 1998, it had a 440-horsepower version of Chevrolet's LS1 5.7-liter V-8. The C12's introduction shoved Callaway Cars across the threshold from Corvette super tuner to manufacturer of Corvette-derived automobiles.

Each Callaway C12 actually started out as a new Corvette that was completely disassembled in the transformation to an exotic luxury sports car. After disrobing the stock car of all its exterior body parts, Callaway replaced them with a set of swoopy new panels built up from aerospace composites including Kevlar, S-Glass, and carbon fiber. Callaway Competition in Leingarten, Germany, produced the body parts and assembled the C12. Leingarten sits about 25 miles north of Stuttgart, the hometown of both Porsche and Mercedes-Benz. Besides building the street version of the C12, Callaway Competition built a C12 R version that raced at Le Mans.

The C12 underwent substantial changes beneath its new composite skin. The new bodywork stretched to a width of 2 meters, the maximum under Le Mans race rules and an increase

The Callaway C12 debuted in 1998 with a 440-horsepower version of the LS1 V-8. *David Newhardt*

As of March 2003, there were less than 30 C12s in the world. This was the only one with a 480 hp engine. Although Callaway has earned a reputation for turbocharged engines, latest motor is aspirated, 'stroked' LS6 that displaces 6.2 liters. (PCP)

Callaway starts life as a production C5 that is disassembled then rebuilt using composite body panels and a revised suspension that includes coil-over shocks and longer suspension arms.

All of the engine work and installation is done in the United States, but the chassis is constructed in Germany by Callaway Competition. The 19-inch wheels cover massive 355-millimeter vented brake discs with four-piston calipers.

of 6 inches over the stock Corvette. As a result, it was necessary to replace the stock upper and lower arms of the Corvette independent four-wheel suspension with longer units of in-house design. Callaway also added its own adjustable coil-over shock setup to supplement the stock transverse leaf springs front and rear. Anti-roll bars, revised suspension geometry, and 19-inch wheels with specially designed Pirelli P Zero Rosso high-performance radials completed the handling improvements. Massive internally ventilated four-wheel brake discs, 355 millimeters in diameter, with quadruple piston calipers added plenty of stopping resistance.

Meanwhile, back at Callaway headquarters in Old Lyme, Connecticut, Jim Jones, the man in charge of Callaway engine development, built the C12's prime mover. Jones had been hot rodding Chevy engines since his teens. He has done everything from building engines for Roger Penske and Mark Donohue when they ruled Trans Am racing during the late 1960s to supplying motors for NASCAR's Richard Childress prior to joining Callaway in 2000. Most recently, Jones massaged the 405-horsepower, 5.7-liter LS6 V-8 of the Corvette Z06 to produce 480 horsepower and, even more impressively, 475 ft-lb of torque.

Jones got all this power without resorting to turbochargers or superchargers. Instead he followed the hot rodder's credo of "there is no substitute for

cubic inches." To this end, a longer stroke forged-steel crankshaft increased displacement to 6.2-liters. Each engine was also "blueprinted" following traditional methods like hand-matched pistons and rods for each cylinder. Jones took full advantage of the latest available technology, using special alloys for the pistons and computer-controlled machines for porting and polishing cylinder heads.

Callaway claimed the latest C12 could go from zero to 60 miles per hour in 4.0 seconds flat. Top speed was said to be 191 miles per hour. Despite the massive amount of available torque, the C12 urged drivers to confidently charge into corners without fear of the rear end breaking loose unexpectedly. The longer suspension arms and revised geometry also gave the steering a nicely weighted feel with precise turn-in that is lacking on a stock Corvette. The Leingarten influence was apparent as the C12's ride, and handling communicates a strong German accent. This was a car that, traffic allowing, could comfortably cruise the autobahn all day at 130 miles per hour.

The C12 price averaged around $200,000 depending on options, but it definitely put Corvette in the highest ranks of world-class super cars.

The precise fit and finish of the exterior carries over into the upgraded interior. Options include a built-in Valentine radar detector that should be mandatory in a car that goes from zero to 60 in 4.0 seconds and can do over 190 miles per hour.

italdesign-giugiaro corvette moray

The Corvette Moray was not really an aftermarket special, but instead a concept car that paid tribute to the Corvette from Italian automotive designers Giorgio Giorgetto and son Fabrizio. Fabrizio's Corvette Z06 provided inspiration for the project. After getting approval from GM to use the Corvette name and logos, Fabrizio began designing and developing the Moray for its debut at the 2003 Geneva Motor Show. According to the Italdesign press release, the thought behind the Moray was to "pay hom-age to the fifty-year era of the Chevrolet Corvette, the supreme symbol of the American sports car."

The name Moray was chosen because the car's protruding nose and grille opening contrasted with its "upraised, cut-off tail," and its curvaceous body contour resembled a moray eel "rippling through sea waters." The side gills added to this impression. Plus it was linked to one of the significant styling traits of the Corvette Stingray.

Fabrizio Giugiaro was inspired by his black Z06 to design a car using C5 mechanicals to pay homage to the American muscle car and the Corvette's 50th anniversary. *Italdesign*

Side gills recall the Mako Shark Corvette concepts and enhance the aquatic theme of the Moray name. Note how the super-model dwarfs the low-slung concept car. *Italdesign*

On the Moray, cameras and a dash-mounted video screen replaced exterior mirrors. The circular lights above the central grille opening were actually bi-xenon headlights.

Italdesign called the Moray a quasi-roadster. The doors opened in a normal fashion, but the side panels of the glass canopy opened gull-wing style and could be unhinged from the polished steel center post that ran from the windshield frame to the rear deck.

The Moray powertrain contained its least exotic components. Underneath this Italian-esque muscle car was an all-American LS6 V-8 mated to a four-speed automatic transmission. Horsepower was said to be "above 400."

Look past the model doing her Tom Petty imitation, and you'll notice the Moray's polished steel central arch that flows from the windshield frame all the way to the rear deck. This arch supports the canopy sides that open in a gull-wing fashion and can be completely removed for open-air motoring. *Italdesign*

LEFT: The rear view gives a better view of the canopy and its central steel arch. The C5's influence on the flowing lines of the body is very apparent from this angle. *Italdesign*

Giorgetto and his son Fabrizio showed sketches to GM officials including Bob Lutz to gain permission to use the Corvette name and logos. The interior builds on the C5 twin-pod concept for driver and passenger. *Italdesign*

1953/2003 commemorative edition

You are not alone if you think the Commemorative Edition C5 produced by Advanced Automotive Technologies (AAT) represents 50 years of Corvette history better than the understated Anniversary Red specials offered by Chevrolet. The Commemorative Edition was commissioned by Magna Steyr, a supplier to GM and other OEMs, in hopes that Chevrolet would give the company the job of manufacturing it as the official anniversary Corvette.

The car appeared in the Magna Steyr booth at the 2001 SEMA show in Las Vegas. Shortly thereafter, GM decided not to accept Magna Steyr's proposal, although some anonymous GM executives were impressed enough to order copies on their own.

Then Steve Pasteiner, president of AAT, came onto the scene. Pasteiner had significant input into the car's final design, and his company built the prototype. Pasteiner had spent 22

The rear view of the Advanced Automotive Technologies (AAT) 1953–2003 Commemorative Edition C5 captures the look of the first Corvette almost to the letter. Despite the difference in size between the earliest and latest Corvette, the styling works perfectly on the larger chassis. *David Newhardt*

AAT's primary business is designing and building prototypes and concept cars for OEMs. Therefore, the fit and finish of the Commemorative Edition is impeccable. The preferred color scheme is white with a red interior, but the car can be done in black and red. There is also a red ZO6 hardtop in existence, but it lacks the grace of the white roadster. *David Newhardt*

This side view shows that Steve Pasteiner, founder of AAT and a former GM designer, got the proportions for the body kit spot on. The conversion costs $29,995 plus a donor C5 convertible or hardtop. Ninety-nine percent of the job is removing old exterior panels and trim and bolting on new parts. Since it is done by hand, it takes some time. *David Newhardt*

The 1950s theme of the interior employs a two-tone effect on the steering wheel and lower trim. Each car receives a plaque with build number, but AAT does not plan to limit production. *David Newhardt*

years at GM where he became an assistant chief designer for Buick and Chevrolet before founding his design and prototype firm in 1989. AAT works closely with all of the Big Three in the design and building of prototypes and concept cars such as the Buick Blackhawk.

Pasteiner acquired the rights to sell and build the Commemorative Edition. He charged $29,995 plus a donor C5 convertible or hardtop. All new body panels were installed using the same attachment locations as the standard production panels. Modifications were limited to a small recess cut inside the rear trunk to provide clearance for the contour of the new deck lid. This was surprising considering that the parts list included a new inner and outer hood, front fascia, headlights and turn signals, side marker lights, chrome diecast grille and bumpers, rear quarter panels, rear fascia, inner and outer deck lid, chrome diecast rear bumpers, LED taillights and center-

high-mounted-stop-light (CHMSL), custom exhaust tips, high intensity backup lights, chrome five-spoke wheels, red painted calipers, and a complete interior do-over including a personalized name and number plate. The preferred color scheme was pearl white with red/white interior, but other color schemes were available on request.

The cars were virtually hand assembled and required the full-time efforts of 10 workers for a week to complete. Pasteiner said he'll make the cars as long as there is sufficient customer demand. As of this writing, there were 39 cars accounted for on an independent Web site devoted to the 53/03 Commemorative Edition.

The car's workmanship appeared to be better than what rolls out of Bowling Green, with no slam intended at current C5 quality. In terms of its appearance and charisma, there was no argument that this was the real 50th anniversary Corvette.

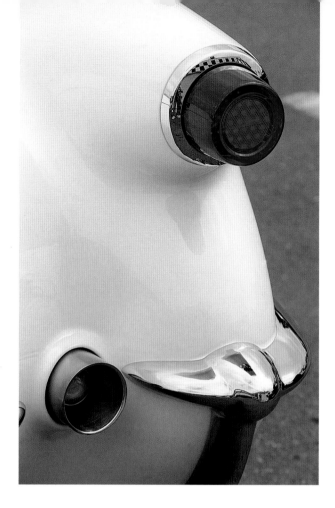

This car is a mass of gentle curves and interesting details. A circle of bright LEDs lights up the taillights. Faux exhaust pipes protruding through the rear fascia house the back-up lights, which have a bluish cast. *David Newhardt*

mallett hammer

Mallett Cars was founded in 1997 specifically to provide performance tuning and parts for the C5 Corvette. By then, brothers Chuck and Lance Mallett had already established a decade-long reputation at Mallett Motorsports for building fast and capable handling Corvettes for the World Challenge and Trans-Am racing series.

The Mallett 435 was the *ne plus ultra* Corvette conversion. It featured an LS1/LS6 V-8 that was stroked to "square" dimensions (3.90-inch bore x 3.90-inch stroke) for a displacement of 6.1 liters (372-ci for old school hot rodders). Mallett claimed that a square engine, in which bore and stroke measure the same, provided more torque. The longer stroke was achieved with a custom billet 4340 chromoly crankshaft, connecting rods of the same material, and custom ceramic coated forged pistons. The heads were ported, matched, and cc'd. Compression was bumped to a ratio of 11.5:1. The result was 500 horsepower 5,800 rpm and 500 ft-lb of torque at 4,800 rpm.

Dan Adovasio is president of the C5 Registry, an enthusiast group with about 7,000 members dedicated to the fifth-generation Corvette. Willing to do anything for the cause, Adovasio turned over his brand new 2002 Z06 to Charlie Mallett for a Hammer massage treatment that consisted of new shocks, exhaust, suspension settings, and engine work that added roughly 70 horsepower at the rear wheels. The graphics were applied by the C5 Registry, which plans to showcase the car at various club functions. *Walt Thurn*

Other goodies in the $33,000, 435 conversion package included a stainless-steel exhaust system, Penske Indy Style double-adjustable shock absorbers, tubular front and rear stabilizer bars, Mallett five-spoke forged three-piece 18-inch wheels (9.5 inch wide fronts, 11 inch wide rears), Michelin Pilot Sport tires (265/35 front, 295/35 rear), leather seats, billet aluminum sport shifter, assorted emblems and logos, and a Mallett serial number.

Like all Corvette enthusiasts, the Mallett people recently turned their focus toward the Z06. The Mallett Hammer could pound out 475 horsepower from the basically stock LS6 without extensive internal modifications. The $12,500 package employed old school hot rodder tricks like porting the heads, which were also flow matched and cc checked. Custom valve springs and lightweight retainers kept the valvetrain under control at high revs. Stainless steel long-tube headers finished off the engine mods.

Also included with the basic Hammer package were a billet shifter, non-adjustable Penske shock absorbers, and the prerequisite, attention-grabbing graphics and logos to impress those who may miss the subtlety of a 475-horsepower Z06.

Mallett was serious about probing the performance limits of the C5. And this was obvious in the performance and handling of its vehicles.

Lingenfelter LPE Twin Turbo Corvette

Lingenfelter Performance Engineering has been turning out extremely fast Chevrolets and other GM vehicles for over 25 years. Instead of taking the normally aspirated path followed by Mallett, LPE has concentrated on turbochargers and superchargers to make horsepower. Their latest project car used a special 7.0-liter, aluminum C5-R block and twin turbos to make 725 horsepower and a massive 650 ft-lb of torque.

The more conservative LPE approach used the stock LS1 of the C5 and got 550 horsepower with the assist of twin turbos. Here is a driving impression written a couple of years ago after this author got to experience a mere 500-horsepower version LPE C5:

Unless the Mulsanne Straight is part of your daily commute, you may never see the 206 miles per hour that the people at Lingenfelter Performance Engineering did when they took their Twin Turbo Corvette to the test track. Odds are you'll run out of road or courage long before you run out of horsepower. But that's not to say you'll never have a chance to get acquainted with every one of those 500 horses under the hood.

How easy is it to start a stampede? Take a nice, easy-rolling start then drop the throttle and hang on. The turbos are ready to rock around 1,500 rpm, and you better be ready to react to some serious horsepower production.

Whoa! We were immediately at full gallop, knocked back in the seat, working the six-speed transmission to cope with the tach needle that seemed magnetically attracted to the red zone. At least we weren't as dazed and confused as the computer system assigned to herding all this acceleration in a somewhat straight line.

Trampled in the sudden rush of tire-twisting horsepower, the traction control decided to jump off as we shifted to second. Maybe its little, electric brain thought it felt the landing gear going up and assumed we had taken off. You can't blame it for being fooled.

What was once a wide-open highway had, in seconds, become filled with traffic that appeared to be moving backward at a furious pace. We had to rein in the Corvette and rejoin the herd of daily drivers. The Twin Turbo didn't mind, but that handful of seconds at full thrust certainly got our attention, even though the LPE Twin Turbo had barely tapped 50 percent of its speed potential.

And that's what makes this car so impressive, especially for a Corvette that's been massaged by the aftermarket. Let's face it, normally a 500-horsepower 'Vette is about as subtle as a hand grenade. But don't let the cop-baiting purple graphics on this one fool you. Even though it puts up numbers like zero to 60 in 3.8 seconds and 7.7 seconds to 100 miles per hour, the equally impressive side of the equation is that you can drive it in traffic and around town without hassles or compromises.

As a testament to the basic solidity of the C5, the car we drove was still in fine fettle despite being a 1997 that had led its entire life as a test mule for three generations of engine testing programs. The Twin Turbo's predecessor, the normally aspirated 383-ci powerplant Lingenfelter, had put out 450 horsepower.

Lingenfelter had to work hard on that engine to get that much power, resorting to major internal changes to the crankshaft, rods, pistons, and camshaft. The Twin Turbo, on the other hand, achieved its 500 horsepower and matching 500 ft-lb of torque without any internal modifications to the engine. LPE commends the Chevy engineers who worked on the LS-1 for doing a thorough job of building an efficient, well-designed powerplant. They praise the motor's even air-to-fuel distribution from cylinder to cylinder—which means there is little variation in the spark required by each cylinder. Turbocharging such an engine means you can go against conventional wisdom and avoid lowering the compression ratio or backing off the timing. As a result, boost pressure can be kept very manageable, less than 5 pounds, and the engine's operating temperature remains in the 210 to 220 degree range.

LEFT: LPE claimed zero to 60 in under 4.0 seconds for this 500-horsepower car. Twin turbos begin to spool up around 1,500 rpm, and after that things get real crazy, real fast. This photo shows the car doing some of the first hot laps (actually semi-hot laps) at Irwindale Speedway before the grandstand was finished. *David Newhardt*

PREVIOUS PAGES: The Lingenfelter Twin Turbo C5 has more than wild graphics to attract the cops. The older version had 500 horsepower, but LPE has boosted that to 550 horsepower. If that's not enough, a 7.0-liter C5-R motor can get you 725 horsepower. *David Newhardt*

The most creative use of a Z06 engine (plus the taillights, door handles, and upper suspension arms) has to be the Mosler MT900. It's basically a 1,980-pound racer that you can, if you are brave and deaf, also drive on the street. The MT900 mounts its 435-horsepower engine amidships in a composite tub with chrome-moly subframes fore and aft. Mosler claims a top speed in excess of 200 miles per hour and a rocket ship ride from zero to 60 miles per hour in 3.5 seconds. *Tory Kooyman*

The Mosler rides on 18-inch wheels and stands a little over 3-1/2 feet high. Prices start at $159,000. *Tory Kooyman*

LPE worked hard to find a way to install the turbos. The only place they fit was tucked down below the front of the engine. This necessitated casting special four-into-one exhaust manifolds with housings to mount the turbos. The turbos sit so low that LPE had to devise a way to scavenge oil out of the turbos and back up into the oil pan. The turbos are modified Garrett of Japan units that have low-friction ball bearings allowing them to spool up quickly even with less than 5 pounds of boost.

Additional plumbing was required for the two high-efficiency intercoolers that sit just forward of the front wheel wells. When you open the hood, the only visible signs of all this extra plumbing are the custom air ducts and the bright blue water lines for the intercoolers.

It's hard to improve on the stock C5 handling, so LPE followed the factory's lead and added Z51 front and rear springs and anti-sway bars.

The test car carried over $10,000 worth of brakes, but if you are going to drive a car that goes 196 miles per hour (rpm limited in fifth gear: the optional 3.15 will get you to 206), you better be able to stop it. The pizza-pan-sized, 14-inch, two-piece rotors at all four wheels with Baer/Alcon six-piston calipers in front and four-piston units in the rear should do this very nicely.

appendix

C5 PRODUCTION

YEAR	COUPE	CONVERTIBLE	HARDTOP
1997	9,752	-	-
1998	19,235	11,849	-
1999	18,078	11,161	4,031
2000	18,113	13,479	2,090
2001	15,681	14,173	5,768 (Z06)
2002	14,760	12,710	8,297 (Z06)
2003	12,812	14,022	8,635 (Z06)

Source: Chevrolet Communications
• 2003 totals include 11,632 50th Anniversary cars, of which 7,547 were convertibles and 4,085 coupes.

C5 BASE PRICES

YEAR	COUPE	CONVERTIBLE	HARDTOP
1997	$37,495	-	-
1998	$37,995	$44,425	-
1999	$39,171	$45,579	$38,777
2000	$39,475	$45,900	$38,900
2001	$40,475	$47,000	$47,500 (Z06)
2002	$41,450	$47,975	$50,150 (Z06)
2003	$43,895	$50,370	$51,155 (Z06)
2004	$44,535	$51,535	$52,385 (Z06)

Source: Chevrolet Communications

C5-R RACING HISTORY

1999

DATE	TRACK	RACE SERIES	FINISH IN CLASS
1/31/99	Daytona	USRRC	2nd, 12th
3/20/99	Sebring	ALMS	4th, 7th
9/19/99	Road Atlanta	ALMS	4th, 5th
10/10/99	Laguna Seca	ALMS	2nd
11/7/99	Las Vegas	ALMS	3rd

2000

DATE	TRACK	RACE SERIES	FINISH IN CLASS
2/6/00	Daytona	Grand Am	2nd, DNF
3/19/00	Sebring	ALMS	5th, 6th
6/17/00	Le Mans	FIA	3rd, 4th
8/6/00	Mosport	ALMS	2nd
9/2/00	Texas Motor Speedway	ALMS	1st
9/30/00	Road Atlanta	ALMS	1st, 3rd
10/15/00	Laguna Seca	ALMS	2nd, 4th
10/29/00	Las Vegas	ALMS	3rd, DNF

2001

DATE	TRACK	RACE SERIES	FINISH IN CLASS
2/3/01	Daytona	Grand Am	1st, 2nd
3/4/01	Texas Motor Speedway	ALMS	1st, 4th
3/17/01	Sebring	ALMS	2nd, 3rd
6/16/01	Le Mans	ACO	1st, 2nd
7/22/01	Sears Point	ALMS	1st, 2nd
8/4/01	Portland	ALMS	1st, DQ
8/19/01	Mosport	ALMS	1st, 3rd
8/25/01	Mid-Ohio	ALMS	1st, 2nd
9/9/01	Laguna Seca	ALMS	2nd, 3rd
10/9/01	Road Atlanta	ALMS	1st

2002

DATE	TRACK	RACE SERIES	FINISH IN CLASS
3/16/02	Sebring	ALMS	1st, 4th
5/19/02	Sears Point	ALMS	1st, 2nd
6/15/02	Le Mans	ACO	1st, 2nd
6/30/02	Nid-Ohio	ALMS	1st, 2nd
7/7/02	Road America	ALMS	1st, 2nd
7/21/02	Washington D.C.	ALMS	1st, 2nd
8/3/02	Trois Rivieres	ALMS	2nd, 4th
8/18/02	Mosport	ALMS	1st, 2nd
9/22/02	Laguna Seca	ALMS	3rd, DNF
10/5/02	Miami	ALMS	1st, 2nd
10/12/002	Road Atlanta	ALMS	1st, 3rd
Source: General Motors			

2003

DATE	TRACK	RACE SERIES	FINISH IN CLASS
3/15/03	Sebring	ALMS	1st, 3rd
6/14/03	Le Mans	ACO	2nd, 3rd
6/29/03	Road Atlanta	ALMS	1st, 3rd
7/27/03	Infineon	ALMS	1st, 2nd
8/3/03	Trois Rivieres	ALMS	1st, 2nd
8/17/03	Mosport	ALMS	1st, 7th
8/24/03	Road America	ALMS	2nd, 5th
9/7/03	Laguna Seca	ALMS	2nd, 3rd
9/27/03	Miami	ALMS	4th, DNS
10/15/03	Road Atlanta	ALMS	3rd, 5th

bibliography

RESOURCE directory

All Corvettes Are Red: Inside the Rebirth of an American Legend
James Schefter
1996, Simon & Schuster, Inc.

The Corvette Black Book, 1953-2001
2000, Michael Bruce Associates, Inc.

Corvette C5
Mike Mueller
1998, MBI Publishing Company

Corvette: America's Sports Car
Randy Leffingwell
1997, MBI Publishing Company

Corvette: Fifty Years
Randy Leffingwell
2002, MBI Publishing Company

National Corvette Museum
350 Corvette Drive, Bowling Green, KY 42101-9134
270-781-7973
www.corvettemuseum.com

The C5 Registry
P.O. Box 541023
Merritt Island, FL 32954-1023
321-452-2743
www.c5registry.com

Bondurant School of High Performance Driving
P.O. Box 51980
Phoenix, AZ 85076-1980
800-842-7223
www.bondurant.com

Advanced Automotive Technologies
1763 West Hamlin Road
Rochester Hills, MI 48309
248-852-2900
www.aatcars.com

Callaway Companies
3 High Street
Old Lyme, CT 06371
860-434-9002
www.callawaycars.com

Guldstrand Motor Productions, LLC
805 S. San Fernando Blvd.
Burbank, CA 91502
818-567-1600
www.CorvetteThunder.com

Lingenfelter Performance Engineering
1557 Winchester Road
Decatur, IN 46733
260-724-2552
www.lingenfelter.com

Mallett Cars Inc.
484 Geiger Street
Berea, OH 44017
440-243-8550
www.mallettcars.com

Mosler Automotive
2391 Old Dixie Highway
Riviera Beach, FL 33404
561-842-2492
www.moslerauto.com

index

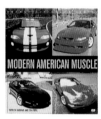